Creating World Champions

STEPHAN SCHMIDT & TIM STEGMANN

CREATING WORLD CHAMPIONS

HOW GERMAN SOCCER WENT FROM SHAMBLES TO CHAMPIONS

Meyer & Meyer Sport

Original title: **Im Glanz des vierten Sterns**, Meyer & Meyer Verlag Aachen, 2015
Translation: AAA Translation, St. Louis, Missouri

British Library Cataloguing in Publication Data
A catalogue record for this book is available from the British Library

Creating World Champions
Maidenhead: Meyer & Meyer Sport (UK) Ltd., 2016
ISBN 978-1-78255-093-8

Aachen, Auckland, Beirut, Cairo, Cape Town, Dubai, Hägendorf, Hong Kong,
Indianapolis, Manila, New Delhi, Singapore, Sydney, Tehran, Vienna

 Member of the World Sport Publishers' Association (WSPA)

Manufacturing: Print Consult GmbH, Munich
E-Mail: info@m-m-sports.com
www.m-m-sports.com

CONTENTS

PART 3: EXAMPLES

PART 4: AMATEUR SOCCER

PREFACE

In recent years, a team was formed from exceptionally well-trained players that rightfully won the world championship title in Brazil. Thus, a success was created whose foundation and development I was able to closely follow at various clubs during my time as a professional soccer coach in Germany. Starting at the turn of the millennium, the DFB (German Soccer Association) set the decisive course for today's success with its support program for soccer talent and its youth performance centers. It is the reason why today the Bundesliga is the best league in the world, the number one, 100%.

My own work as a coach is very much shaped by youth soccer. During my own pro soccer career, I coached PSV Eindhoven's U15 players and later became PSV's youth coordinator. No matter where I subsequently coached pro soccer, I always have and still do watch the games of the respective youth teams as a matter of course, and in recent years, I have noticed an enormous increase in quality.

German soccer has always placed importance on a strong body and positive mindset, but the decisive factor, namely the ball, was gradually installed as the foundation pillar in training center philosophy: ball control, solving different game situations, and creativity with the ball. These are just a few important elements that should be emphasized in training.

It was also important to think outside the box and find inspiration from other soccer nations. The prerequisite for this success is learning from others and thereby improving oneself.

The foundation for pro soccer is training, which is where qualifications are created. Of course, let's not forget that we professional coaches also profit. My younger fellow coaches in the Bundesliga, who in some cases completed their own training in the youth performance centers, are further proof of this positive development.

While the introduction of the U17 and U19 Junior Bundesliga has created a high performance level and, of course, everyone wants to win, the first priority should always be the training of players rather than the result. Titles aren't that important in youth soccer. What matters is content.

Irrespective of the fast pace of day-to-day business in pro soccer, development and continuity are the defining features. Youth soccer is about the future. All the work done in youth soccer must be future-oriented.

This book provides us with an excellent insight into the training philosophy of different Bundesliga teams and teaches us about the diversity and complexity of talent development. Moreover, it shows us the different paths of players. These examples are proof that performance fluctuations and setbacks can already occur during youth training and that it is not always the biggest talents who become successful professionals.

Talent is a prerequisite, but you must constantly prove yourself and can never become complacent. Rather, you must possess the ambition, tenacity, and will to continue to improve. I would like for young players to muster the necessary patience in spite of their ambition. Even when you get tons of praise from lots of people after a couple of good games, you must still keep your feet firmly on the ground.

But mistakes should and must be made, especially while young, because we learn from them. Only then can you take the next step, and it increases the likelihood of achieving your goals.

I hope you enjoy this book!

Huub Stevens

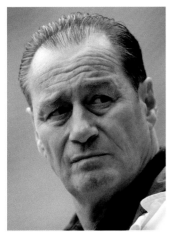

Huub Stevens, long-time Bundesliga coach at VfB Stuttgart, Hamburger SV, Schalke 04, 1. FC Köln, and Hertha BSC

INTRODUCTION

INTRODUCTION

On July 13, 2014, along with friends and approximately 37 million other German viewers, we intently watched the World Cup final in Brazil against Argentina. Between snacks and the large screen, the viewers regularly held their breath as they eagerly followed the team into extra time. Shortly after Mario Götze scored the decisive goal, it was finally done. After 24 years, the German national team had won the World Cup again and created an unparalleled euphoria in the land. A young German national team enthused with its creative, offensive soccer was the only team to find that perfect blend of individual skills and teamwork.

Mario Götze decides the 2014 World Cup final.

Their incomparable style was impressive! The players' concentration, their confident but never arrogant statements, and the team's joy and simultaneous humility were exemplary.

CREATING WORLD CHAMPIONS

Children proudly wear jerseys with the names Müller, Neuer, and those of other World Cup stars. Soccer clubs are barely able to withstand the onslaught of enthusiastic young players who want to emulate their famous role models.

And as cheering fans of this team, we were right in the thick of it. The ease with which Lahm and company raised the trophy to the night sky—these are unforgettable moments captured by countless photos. But what we cannot see in those photos is the arduous and difficult path German soccer has been on for more than a decade in order to reach this success.

Once the emotions gradually subsided after the World Cup triumph and the tournament underwent a more sober analysis, one point became distinctly obvious. While looking at the team makeup of the German World Cup squad, it became apparent that World Cup record holder, Miroslav Klose, is quite unique in his career: He is the only one who was not trained at a youth performance center. Also of note: The players trained at a number of very different youth performance centers at Germany's soccer clubs—different from the previous model, Spain, where training is concentrated in just a few clubs like FC Barcelona, Real Madrid, Atlético Bilbao, and San Sebastian.

A total of 60 clubs participated in the development of the world champions, including 27 licensed clubs and 33 amateur organizations.

The world cup is the crowning glory of Germany's unparalleled talent development over the past decade. Bundesliga clubs count on their young talent. The young players are the winners and at the same time profit from the positive changes in German soccer. It was different just 15 years ago. Hardly anyone raved about the new generation of German soccer talent. In most professional teams, it was revolutionary to have two 19-year-olds on the squad on game day. Even if there were some changes over time, the development of youth players became a steady trend. More and more clubs bank on their own talent, who are becoming increasingly younger and very well trained.

The combination of athletic and academic training as well as full educational, medical, and psychological support for young German players has become a model for international soccer.

The soccer world is amazed by the virtually inexhaustible reserve of talented young players in Germany. Training "made in Germany" is once again a quality guarantee.

In recent years, coaches, fathers, mothers, friends, children, and adolescents, as well as acquaintances that are sports enthusiasts have been asking lots of questions on this topic. How does a Bundesliga club's youth performance center operate? How did this turnabout, this extensive rethinking in German clubs with respect to youth players, happen?

Why do many players who appear to be less talented than others make it in pro soccer? Under which conditions do the talents train? Why are many players unable to make the leap to pro soccer? What are clubs doing differently today from 10 years ago? What does a top player do to play at the highest level long term? These are just a few questions we will try to answer in this book.

We want to show a timeline of the changes that have taken place since 2000 and how the youth performance centers have organically evolved since that time. How do the academies of Bundesliga clubs like Borussia Dortmund, Hertha BSC, VfB Stuttgart, and VfL Wolfsburg prepare their talent for pro soccer? We will talk about the difficult balancing act during the transition period after the end of U19, as well as take a look at the different paths of some star players. Marco Reus, Shkodran Mustafi, Maximilian Arnold, Manuel Neuer, and Sebastian Rode provide an insight into their inner life and their different career progressions. Moreover, some of them will demonstrate through select training units how to work every day on strengths and weaknesses in order to rise to the top.

Because next to fundamental skills, will, and luck, it also requires day-to-day work to make the break to the top. Pro soccer would not be possible without amateur soccer; therefore we will finally take a look at it. Individual topics will be presented with input from recognized German soccer experts.

Our goal was to give the reader a better understanding of the transition in German soccer by providing answers.

When we say we, we refer to all the people whose cooperation made this book possible. Many thanks for your support and your uncomplicated nature, safe in the knowledge that the everyday business of soccer is fast-paced and difficult. In the course of countless interesting conversations, many interesting perspectives emerged, which we will share with the reader in the following chapters. We hope all of you will enjoy this book!

PART 1: LOOKING BACK

1
THE DANCING REFRIGERATORS[1]

–FROM THE DEPRESSION OF THE TURN OF THE MILLENIUM TO THE FOURTH TITLE

In 2000, German soccer was in ruins. A generation that supposedly would be invincible for years to come presented as too old—in fact, the term "Stone Age soccer" came to mind. The proud German soccer nation was deeply depressed. Did not the German national team just founder 0-3 with "grandpa style"[2] against a Portuguese B-team? Two years prior, the German national team already rumbled into the 1998 World Cup quarter-finals not with inspired soccer, but rather with the internationally much feared "German virtues." But then it was over. The team lost to Croatia 0-3. Fitness and fight were no longer enough. But other nations played inspiring soccer.

There was no trace of young, exciting soccer players inspiring joy of play and enthusiasm with their speed and readiness for action.

And all this at a most inconvenient time! The 2006 World Cup at home was fast approaching, and the soccer powerhouse Germany fell into

---

1   Quote after *ft* Sept., 2010, p. 6.
2   Weekly newspaper, *Die Zeit*, May 5, 2011 (No. 19), p. 18.

pieces. The contrast between pretense and reality could not have been greater. Germany, which held a permanent claim to leadership in world soccer since 1954, appeared to have been relegated to Stone Age soccer.

Devastated—the German team at the 2000 European Championship after losing 0-3 to a Portuguese B-team

Germany's self-image in soccer changed. Instead of being "unbeatable for years to come," German soccer was quickly struck by a hard reality.[3] Winning while also playing attractive soccer—that's what others did. France (world champions 1998, European champions 2000), the Netherlands, and especially Spain were vanguards of youth development. Looking beyond one's borders was beneficial. German soccer profited greatly from the experience and skills of the acquired knowledge regarding approach, strategy, and training and put together a talent support program without equal. Inspiration was also gained from other sports such as ice hockey and team handball.

In 1998, the state associations already received 2 million DM from the DFB to ramp up development of 11- to 12-year-olds.[4] In addition, the DFB built 120 support centers all

---

3   *Sport Bild*. Available at: http://sportbild.bild.de/meine-meinung/2014.meine-meinung/u19-triumph-ein-titel-ohne-bayern-37062756.sport.html. Oct. 8, 2014
4   Schott on *ft*, September, 2010, Talent Development, p. 7.

over Germany for 3.2 billion DM for additional support for 13- to 17-year-old talent.[5] Prior to that it had been left to the individual state associations and clubs to engage in talent development as they saw fit. At that time, there was no concept for an integrated approach.[6]

1.1 THE FIRST STEP–AN EXTENSIVE NETWORK OF DFB CENTERS

The provisional talent program remained in this form until 2001. After the disastrous 2000 European Championship, two decisive advances in talent development in Germany took place with the mandatory institution of performance centers for Bundesliga clubs in 2001, as well as the construction of 366 base camps.[7] The DFB base camps form a close-meshed, comprehensive network all over Germany, allowing 1,000 base camp coaches to sight nearly every talent and invite them to the base camp. Base camp training begins at the so-called golden age of learning, age 11. A total of 14,000 players get the opportunity once a week to work on their weaknesses and develop their strengths during an additional training session.[8] For most of the talent, the base camps are thereby the first step in their soccer development. At the same time, the base camps are catch basins for all talent in the event they withdraw from a performance center.

---

5   Ibid.
6   Ibid.
7   Schott on *ft*, Sept, 2010, Talent Development, p. 8
8   DFB online talent development. Available at: *http://talente.dfb.de/index.php?id=519131*; Schott, 2010, Talent development as a success factor: Evaluation of DFB talent development with a view to the 2010 world cup, *ITK*, p. 57.

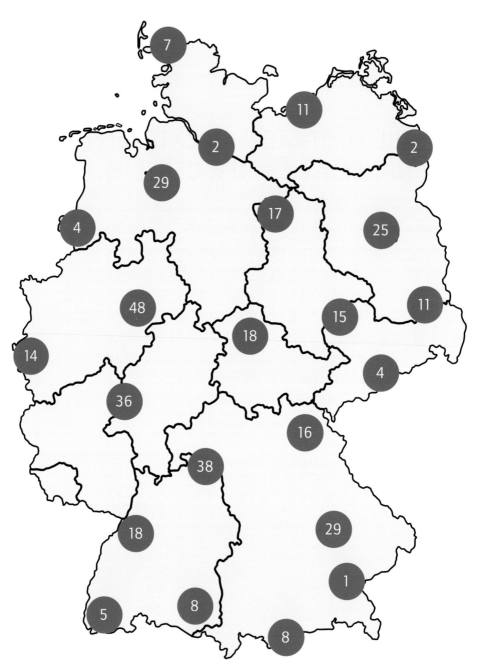

Map of Germany showing DFB base camps

The talent with the presumably best prospects switch from the base camp to a performance center. All players who are not yet playing at a performance center by the end of the base camp age limit of age 14 receive additional support from the state association to enable the switch to a youth academy at a later date.[9] Stefan Kießling, Dennis Aogo, Mario Gómez, Toni Kroos, and André Schürrle are just a few of the players who made the switch from a base camp to a performance center. Dennis Aogo, Mario Gómez, and Stefan Kießling even did so relatively late.[10]

DFB talent development program

Bambini (U7)[11]

MOVEMENT – JOY

- Holistic support of children through movement tasks.

- Playful learning about the flying, bouncing, and rolling the ball.

- A variety of ideas and joy of playing through variations of small ball games.

- Joy of playing (soccer).

- Learning simple basic rules of playing with and against each other.

U8/U9[12]

- Small groups, small fields, lots of activities.

- Training is playing with lots of touches for everyone.

- Promote playing with both feet, creativity, and joy of playing.

- Promote learning through the demonstrate–imitate method.

- Show patience; no time–performance pressure.

- Set an example for the children at all times.

---

9   Schott on *ft*, September, 2010, p. 9.
10 *fussballtraining*, September, 2010, p. 10-11.
11 *DFB training approach*. Available at: http://fussballtraining.com/blaetterfunktion/ausbildungskonzeption/files/assets/basic-html/page16.html.
12 *DFB training approach*. Available at: http://fussballtraining.com/blaetterfunktion/ausbildungskonzeption/files/assets/basic-html/page19.html.

U10/U11[13]

- Promote individual strengths.

- Technical training is primarily playing.

- Strive for lots of touches and playing activity for everyone.

- Emphasize accurate progressions; correct when necessary.

- Teach tactical basic ABCs.

- Demonstrate fairness, dependability, and politeness.

U12/U13[14]

- Improve all basic techniques step-by-step and in detail.

- Combine practicing and playing with emphasis on both.

---

13   *DFB Ausbildungskonzeption*, p. 20. Available at: http://fussballtraining/blaetterfunktion/ausbildungskonzeption/files/ assets/basic-html/page20.html.

14   Ibid.

- Enforce the use of both feet.

- Train fitness primarily through games.

- Begin individual training.

- Use intensive communication, actively involving players.

U14/U15[15]

- Be aware of differences in individual development.

- Individual support: strengthen strengths, weaken weaknesses.

- Build and strengthen self-initiative and self-motivation.

- Creativity is more important than rigid tactical processes.

- No premature position specialization.

- Build hierarchies; create responsibilities.

U16/U17 and U18/U19[16]

- Provide intensive training processes and active breaks.

- Train technical–tactical details in theory and practice.

- Make training more complex, but consider individuality.

- Actively involve players; facilitate participation in decision making.

- Build a hierarchical structure within the team.

- Coordinate athletic and academic demands.

---

15   Ibid.
16   *DFB Ausbildungskonzeption*, p. 26. Available at: http://fussballtraining/blaetterfunktion/ausbildungskonzeption/files/assets/basic-html/page26.html.

1.2 TALENT DEVELOPMENT AT YOUTH PERFORMANCE CENTERS

The youth performance centers of Bundesliga clubs start the development of young talent at different age groups. Some already begin at the end of U9, but no German academy has a team later than U12. In the youth performance centers, the younger players (U13 and U15) train four to six times a week; the older players (U17 and U19) train six to eight times a week.[17] The skills offensive continues with the coaches. Of the 650 coaches total, 271 coach full time. Of these, far more than 50% hold at least a national B license.[18] Matthias Sammer, former DFB athletic director, says, "More than ever, the head coach is the key to and the measure of all things. He takes personal responsibility for the management of individual and team elite support."

Tough rivalry already exists in youth soccer

With the introduction of the U19 Bundesliga during the 2003/2004 season, the U17 Junior Bundesliga in 2007/2008, and the U15 Junior regional league, which competed for the first time in all regions of Germany in 2010-2011, the preconditions were created for performance comparisons between youth performance centers organized as leagues. This way the performance center talent must prove themselves week after week and advance their skills in competition.

---

17   Schött. 2010. *ITK*, p. 57.
18   See Certification. Analysis of performance centers, p. 28 in *DFL*, 2011.

1.3 STAR WARS–ENSURING QUALITY AT YOUTH PERFORMANCE CENTERS

Furthermore, the performance centers are subject to certification by the German Soccer Association (DFB) and German Soccer League (DFL). In doing so, the eight categories *administrative policy and strategy; organization; basic product: soccer training, support, internal marketing, and personnel management; external contacts and recruitment; infrastructure; and, finally, effectiveness are reviewed.*[19] Regular review by the DFB and DFL does not only ensure quality but also regular improvement of Germany's youth performance centers since the standards for youth performance centers in Germany are continuously rising.[20] The company Footpass issues certifications and up to three stars that also carry with them a financial reward so that effective youth development is profitable, especially for less financially well-to-do clubs.

For performance centers, collaborating with schools is essential for optimal talent development. All-day school greatly limits afternoon practice time. The elite soccer academies instituted by the DFB since 2007 make it possible to also have training units in the mornings as well as providing students who miss school due to select training courses flexible opportunities to make up missed work.[21]

1.4 REFORMATION 2.0

But after the shipwreck around the turn of the millennium, it took the reformer Jürgen Klinsmann to break open the inflexible methods of operation within the Bundesliga and raise awareness for new issues. For instance, in Germany in 2008, ball contact times (one of the indicators of a fast game) were still at an average 1.9 seconds. In England's Premier League, where absolute star players have been romping for many years, the ball contact time of top teams was at 1 second.[22]

---

19 Schaukens, Van Hoecke, Simm, and Lochmann. 2008. Certification of performance centers 2007-2008, *ITK*, p. 42.
20 The beginnings. The founding of performance centers, p. 9; Certification. An analysis of performance centers. *DFL*, 2011, p. 26.
21 *DFB, Elite soccer academies.* Available at: http://talente.dfb.de/index.php?id=518840; Rettig, 2011, It must be possible to have a Bundesliga career and a university entrance diploma, *DFL*, p. 12.
22 Gieselmann, 2008, England is miles ahead, *11 Freunde*.

The German national team was already able to reach that number by the 2010 World Cup.[23] Even with regard to modern performance diagnostics, lobbying was still required in 2009 when many other top international coaches had already incorporated this component into their mode of operation.[24]

Initially sneered at, now frequently copied. The American physical team creates new impulses, here with an exercise using elastic bands.

1.5 VISIBLE PROGRESS

For the Bundesliga, the effects are obvious. While 92% of all players used during the 2000/2001 season were still older than age 21, that number dropped to 84% during the 2009/2010 season.[25] Overall, more than 50% of current Bundesliga players were trained at a performance center.[26] On average, that is 15 players per club.[27] Since the 2001/2002 season, the average age has also gone down.

---

23   Näher, 2014, Spain remains the gold standard: Interview with the national team coach, *Schwarzwälder Bote*.
24   Gartenschläger and Schramm, 2009, Why Löw wants DFB players to get a move on, *Die Welt*.
25   Schott, 2010 Talent development, *ft*, p. 11.
26   Success story. The stars from the performance centers, p. 3 *DFL*, 2011: 10 years of performance centers: Talent development in German elite soccer.
27   Seifert, 2011, The investments will pay off, *DFL*, p. 7.

During the 2010/2011 season, the average age in the Bundesliga was 25.77, and, thus, was barely below the 2001/2002 average age.[28] In 2010, the German squad's average age of 25 in South Africa was already six years below the average age of the German squad at the European Championship in 2000. The average age of the world champions of Brazil 2014 was 25.8, which makes them the fourth youngest team in German World Cup history.[29] Borussia Dortmund's team in 2012, when they won the German Championship, was the youngest ever.[30] In parallel to the decrease in average age, the number of German players in the 1st and 2nd Bundesliga has gone up. In the DFL brochure *10 Years of Performance Centers: Talent Development in German Soccer*, the head of DFL management, Christian Seifert, announced, "In today's Bundesliga 57%, and in the 2nd Bundesliga even 71% of all players are German again."[31]

Schalke's former sports director Horst Heldt points to a positive side effect: "When we groom the players ourselves, we facilitate a close identification with the club and are able to influence their training."[32] Next to a sense of allegiance to the club itself, homegrown players like Thomas Müller, Julian Draxler, and Kevin Großkreutz also provide an enormous identifying factor for the fans who perceive "their" players as being more authentic than other, possibly very expensive, foreign star players for whom the own club may be only a way station to the next club.

Thomas Müller, Julian Draxler, and Kevin Großkreutz

28 Average age diagram, *DFL*, 2011, p. 7.
29 *DFB team with fourth youngest squad in world cup history.* Available at: http://www.wm-2014.net/zahlenspiele-dfb-team-durchschnittsalter-von-258-jahren-12345494.html.
30 http://www.abendblatt.de/sport/article2266453/Borussia-Dormund-2012-Bester-Meister-aller-Zeiten.html
31 Ibid.
32 Vis-à-vis Horst Heldt *N-TV*, March 18, 2014.

1.6 GERMAN IN-HOUSE PRODUCTION: THE LOCAL PLAYER

The local player rule, which became mandatory in the Bundesliga with the 2006/2007 season, supports this development. Starting with the 2008/2009 season, every club must have eight locally trained players under contract.[33] A local player is a player who has trained at least three consecutive years between the ages of 15 and 21 in his own or a German club.[34] An interesting fact: Of the 23 world champions in Brazil, 21 trained at least three years or more at a German youth performance center and thereby qualify as local players.

Juvenescence and most likely a simultaneous increase in quality can most certainly also be predicted in the lower leagues. The multitude of talented, well-trained players that make it to base camp but not much beyond do not only raise the quality of play in all other leagues in which the players will subsequently become active, but also simultaneously lower their average age.

Thus, talent development in Germany does not only create a pool of young talent at the top but also across the sport, which almost certainly will result in higher quality soccer in all leagues.

1.7 TO THE TOP OF THE WORLD

In the space of 10 years, the development of youth players in Germany has changed fundamentally. Since the 2001/2002 season, on average, more than 65 million Euros per year are invested in youth performance centers. With the development of professional structures in youth soccer, regular certification by the DFL, a close-meshed talent support network, as well as DFB base camps, performance centers, and ensuring a comprehensive training process through cooperation between schools and clubs, the foundation was laid for a year-by-year renewable generation of well-trained talent that last summer crowned itself world champion.

---

33   Success Story – the Stars from the Performance Centers, *DFL*, 2011, p. 3; *Bundesliga*. Questions about the business of soccer. Available at: http://www.bundesliga.de/dfl/fragen/.
34   Ibid.; 10 Years of Performance Centers, *DFL*, 2011, p. 39.

Bastian Schweinsteiger, Marco Reus, Philipp Lahm, Thomas Müller, Mesut Özil, Sami Khedira, Manuel Neuer, Mario Götze, Toni Kroos—by now the list of notable star players who came from a youth performance center has become quite long and at the same time forms the core of today's national team. Matthias Sammer, DFB performance director from 2006 to 2012, continually emphasized that the German Soccer Association must orient itself to the world elite.[35] In 2009, the DFB's youth development work was recognized with the UEFA's Maurice Burlaz Trophy as Europe's best. The U21, U19, and U17 European Championship titles of the national teams were instrumental here.[36]

The next generation is ready! Germany's U19 win the European Championship.

Thus, the world championship title is a logical conclusion to the conceptual and structural changes and a product of the investments of the past decade. The entire world now looks to us.

35   *DFB*, DFB honored for best youth development work in Europe. Available at: http://www.dfb.de/index.php?id=500014&tx_dfbnews_pi1%5BshowUid%5D-20992&tx_dfbnews_pi4%5Bcat%5D=70.

36   Ibid.; *Financial Times Germany*, UEFA Recognizes DFB Youth Development Efforts. Available at: http://ftd.de/sport/fussball/nationalmannschaft/:uefa-zeichnet-dfb-nachwuchsarbeit-aus/50028845.html.

TIMELINE 1998-2014	
Markers:	
1998	World Cup in France; 0-3 in quarter-finals against Croatia
1999	Preliminary talent development program
2000	German national team debacle at the European Championship in the Netherlands and Belgium
2001	Construction of DFB base camps and the beginning of an extensive talent development network
2001/2002	Youth performance centers as a stipulation in the licensing process (initially for the 1st Bundesliga)
2002	Expanded talent development program; 2nd Bundesliga performance centers
2004	Again group-stage knock-out at the European Championship
2006	World Cup at home; third place finish

Unfulfilled summer dream—the 2006 World Cup

2006/2007	Local player rule is implemented
2007	Elite soccer academies are established by the DFB
2008	European Championship loss in final against Spain
2008	Optimized talent development program and certification of performance centers

TIMELINE 1998-2014	
2009	DFB youth development receives award
2010	World Cup in South Africa; third place finish
2012	European Championship semi-final elimination against Spain
2013	Two German teams, Bayern Munich and Borussia Dortmund, in Champions League final
2014	WORLD CHAMPIONS in Brazil

PART 1: LOOKING BACK

2

A WORD FROM GERMANY'S TOP COACH–

INTERVIEW WITH FRANK WORMUTH

Frank Wormuth is head coach for the DFB's soccer instructor training course as well as coach for the U20 national team. In preparation for the 2014 World Cup in Brazil, the U20 acted as training partner to the German national A team, and he was on location in Brazil as DFB analyst.

> As head coach of the DFB, you have analyzed the World Cup extensively. What were the key factors for the German team during the tournament for the World Cup title?

"I would say first of all team spirit, because you can only be successful when the entire team selflessly pulls together. The example of Mertesacker after he was taken out of the first squad makes that particularly apparent. The men around Jogi Löw then had a definite game plan that was constantly implemented. Moreover, the players were completely attuned to their opponents. But we cannot forget the team composition, particularly the thoughtful integration of the injured players Schweinsteiger, Klose, and Khedira, and especially the players behind the top 14. They did not cause any upheaval, but rather created a cheerful atmosphere. And as an aside, it should be mentioned that the players as a whole were of high quality."

"ABOVE ALL, THERE IS PLAYING CONTINUITY"

> What can coaches who work in youth performance centers learn from the World Cup and implement in their work?

"Basically these coaches can take anything from the World Cup and implement it in their domain, of course adapted to their level. Why shouldn't youth teams play in different formations during a game or defend with a back five and open the game with a back three?"

> Spain has dominated world soccer for years with three consecutive national team titles. What could the DFB learn from Spain during that time?

"Most of all, possession play. And patience in implementing their game plan even in negative situations, regardless of the voice of the people."

> As a U20 coach in the DFB, you work with players from the U23, 3rd League, 2nd League, and Bundesliga. In your opinion, is there an optimal education for long-term success in pro soccer?

"Above all, there is playing continuity. Of course, it would be advantageous for young players in the highest league to have appearances all the time, but due to the high quality of their colleagues, that isn't always possible. Therefore, it can also be a lower league, but in the end it is just about playing, regardless where. That is why the compromise of training in the Bundesliga and playing in the 2nd League is still better than sitting on the bench at the top."

> During your time as U20 coach, did you invite players to the U20 that were not trained at a youth performance center?

"Since I always evaluate players in the here and now, I did not make a detailed historical analysis of the players I invited. Therefore, I can only respond by instinct, that nearly all of them trained at youth performance centers. At least I have not heard otherwise."

> In international comparisons with the U20, is there a noticeable increase in respect toward Germany?

"That respect has always been there because other countries have always regarded Germany as something special in soccer. After winning the World Cup in Brazil and the worldwide realization that we have a first-class youth training program, the international playing partners are even more eager to win against us. Beating the world champion is the best, even if it is just in a friendly game. Only the Germans can truly lose. That is the flip side of the medal of success."

"BEATING THE WORLD CHAMPION IS THE BEST"

> Are there positions where Germany has deficiencies with respect to youth players and elite soccer?

"It is no secret that we are currently looking for fullbacks and center forwards for our national A team. There might have been too much emphasis on the center of the game during training, or the well-trained players want more contact with the ball and applied for center midfield positions. But one thing I have noticed recently is the fact that the Spanish can still show us a few things in terms of technique under pressure. This requires intensified training at the youth level. We can shift like world champions, double-team and defend high. We are great at system-oriented movement and coordinated running. But we

still have plenty of development potential in basic defensive and offensive behavior. It is about ordinary tackling behavior on defense and offense. The magic word is action speed."

> The experts gush about the German national team's offensive, creative style of play. Were different offensive player types developed in recent years?

"As a result of youth development centers hiring more and more full-time coaches who just focused on soccer all day long, the beneficiaries have been the youth players. They receive professional training, be it through modern live coaching or video analyses. This automatically results in technically and tactically better-trained players."

> The trend is very early integration of talent into professional teams. What is your opinion on this development?

"On the one hand, I see it as a positive since these players improve the game overall because they can also regenerate more quickly. But on the other hand, these young players will have reached their physical peak increasingly earlier. In the past, the end of a player's career was around age 35. Today and in the future, players will have to already retire at age 30, or even younger. Another phenomenon of quantitative and qualitative training will be that many good players won't even reach the top because their competitors are also still young. The broad base will profit from this, which isn't so bad either."

"I STILL SEE UPWARD POTENTIAL IN TRAINING"

> In your opinion, which area of training holds the biggest potential?

"As I said before, the training of our youth players needs to focus more on action speed. With all due respect to discussions about formation, running lanes, and group tactics, at the end of the day, the individual decides the game. And here I still see upward potential in training."

> The DFB's goal continues to be the top of the world. Will there be new developmental trends after this World Cup that might have a long-term effect on the game in the future?

"The World Cup showed us many modes of behavior, which means coaches will exhibit more and more flexibility. When a team changes its basic formation during a game, the opposing coach should know the resulting advantage or disadvantage. Based on that knowledge, he must then decide whether to also change or not. If I were to make a prediction, it would be that midfield pressing will decrease because the amount of effort required for winning the ball with the quality of the opposing players is a negative. It is, therefore, possible that the only two choices will be counter-pressing in the opposing half and falling back from the own penalty area. But that is only an impression from the World Cup in Brazil."

PART 2: YOUTH DEVELOPMENT

3

THE WELLSPRING OF THE FUTURE –

YOUTH PERFORMANCE CENTERS

3.1 INTRODUCTION

He knew whom he had to thank. And he immediately used one of the first opportunities after the party in Rio to acknowledge the makers of the young German national team for their part in the great success.

"Of course the Bundesliga, with its training, played a major part. In 2000 and 2004, German soccer was at the bottom. Back then we were eliminated during the preliminary round. Then they took action. It was said that we needed to invest more in training, that we needed technically better players. We would not have made progress with German virtues alone. We have the clubs' performance centers where they do great work. Sure, I always have to say thank you for that. The title is a product of excellent training in Germany."[37]

---

37   Joachim Löw quoted in *Süddeutsche Zeitung* on July 14, 2014. Available at: http://www.sueddeutsche.de/news/sport/fussball-loew-dieses-gluecksgefuehl-wird-fuer-alle-ewigkeit-bleiben-dpa.um-newsml-dpa-com20090101-140714-99-01247.

It is no secret that Joachim Löw and his entire coaching and support staff did sensational work in Brazil and that is also apparent in his award as FIFA World Coach of the Year. But the starting point for the success in Brazil was a long time ago.

The DFB already sent the second youngest team to the 2010 World Cup with an average age of 25.33. Two years later, at the 2012 European Championship, the Germans fielded the youngest team (average age 24.39). Finally, at the 2014 World Cup, the average age of the German team was 25.8 and at the 2016 European Championship the Germans were the youngest team again.

"Developing youth players has no alternative."[38] **–Matthias Sammer**

The current sport director and former coach of RB Leipzig, Ralf Rangnick, describes the need for a drastic intervention into Germany's youth player development as follows:

"Compared to other international teams we were behind in the tactical area all the way back to the turn of the millennium. But that is not the case anymore. Fifteen years ago, we began to recognize where our problems were. Back then, there were still coaches who believed that tactics were only for bad players. The right impetus came from the youth academies of the clubs and gradually lapped over into pro soccer."[39]

Meanwhile, you can almost set your watch by the breakthrough of the next German youth talent in the German Bundesliga. Maximilian Arnold in Wolfsburg, Julian Brandt in Leverkusen, Marian Sarr at Borussia Dortmund, now in Wolfsburg, Leroy Sané at Schalke 04, Timo Werner at VfB Stuttgart, now in Leipzig, or Gianluca Gaudino, who is taking his first steps at FC Bayern—all of them are products of German youth performance centers. These young players are the face of the Bundesliga, only now there is no new trend. The results of this systematic training are obvious. This is not only true of the players but also of the increasing number of young and successful coaches like Thomas Tuchel, Christian Streich, Julian Nagelsmann, Tayfun Korkut, and Markus Gisdol, who began their meticulous work at the youth performance centers.

---

38 *Focus Online.* Available at: http://www.focus.de/sport/mehrsport/sport-leistung-ist-planbar_aid_569812.html.
39 Ralf Rangnick quoted in the *Stuttgarter Zeitung*, October 25, 2013. Available at: http://www.stuttgarter-zeitung.de/inhalt.ralf-rangnick-im-gespraech-fussball-ist-eine-ehrliche-sportart.7d4bac3f-5831-4549-a5da-a7e6329c.html.

From youth soccer to the pros: Top talent Julian Brandt (Bayer Leverkusen) and coach Christian Streich (SC Freiburg)

But the exchange of ideas and developments is not one-sided. Rather professional and youth soccer inseminate each other in constant communication. Dr. Jens Rehhagel, administrative director of the youth performance center at Hannover 96, explains: "The professional soccer coach introduces videos and content on how he envisions the A team at regularly scheduled advanced training seminars. Talent from our own youth program frequently train with our professional team, and that's when it is helpful to already have certain qualifications in place that are essentially for our professional team. This improves a fluid transition for our talent. But it is also our obligation, and we are asked to also review our own ideas and new developments and integrate them into the daily training process. They must be screened while also working closely with the professional sphere. Regular feedback from the professional coach regarding the talent that trains with him is extremely important. This allows us to seek improvements and work more intensively with the player."

"IN THE END, CHARACTER USUALLY BEATS TALENT"

The goal of youth performance centers is clear: The pros of tomorrow are trained here. Since only a fraction of players can make it in spite of the quality of training, the clubs also assume a great social responsibility. They support education by cooperating with schools, providing tutoring if needed, or offering support in finding a suitable apprenticeship. Frequently bad grades, or worse, bad behavior in school is penalized with training suspension, thereby providing the players with renewed critical focus.

CREATING WORLD CHAMPIONS

Max Eberl, sports director at Borussia Mönchengladbach and previously involved in youth training, states: "Character usually beats talent!"[40]

Frequently, this can be seen in the double burden of school and soccer. Experience tells us, he who can accommodate both and is able to handle everyday life through disciplined self-organization has the best chance of making it. However, Hannover 96 youth performance center director Dr. Jens Rehhagel does not see *that one way*, but lists several reasons for the failure of transitioning talent: "Getting into senior soccer is a major adjustment in all areas. There is more competition, and the market the clubs have access to is global. But it is difficult for me to make a blanket judgment. In my experience, every player has his own story. With some it was more obvious; in others there was a different individual reason why it did not work out. And it is very similar with the positive examples. Most of the time, in individual cases, there was a special set of circumstances that made for the perfect situation."

Youth performance centers make their selections based on the performance principle, even with the youngest teams. This is a very difficult task for coaches and, of course, also is subject to errors in judgment. Not only must they take into account the current status of the talent, but they must also issue prognoses on their future: Which player will be able to play in the world cup in 2022? What qualities will the Bundesliga be looking for in 2018? What does a young talent need to make it all the way to the top? What qualities does the player already possess; what can I teach him; and what will he likely never learn? It is nearly impossible to answer these questions accurately. Nevertheless, each day all responsible parties do all they can to provide the players with the best preparation in terms of technique, tactics, fitness, and personal development for a future not only as a pro soccer player, but also for life.

---

40   *Rp*, Dec. 31, 2012. Available at: http://www.rp-online-de/sport/fussball/borussia/der-charakter-schlaegt-am-ende-meistens-das-talent-ad-1.312--84.

The world champions of Rio 2014

2014 WORLD CUP SQUAD *(FROM LEFT TO RIGHT)*
Manuel Neuer – with Schalke 04 since age 4
Roman Weidenfeller – with 1. FC Kaiserslautern since age 16
Ron-Robert Zieler – with 1. FC Cologne since age 10
Jerome Boateng – with Hertha Berlin since age 14
Phillip Lahm – with FC Bayern Munich since age 12
Erik Durm – with 1. FC Saarbrücken since age 16
Kevin Großkreutz – with Borussia Dortmund since age 14
Mats Hummels – with FC Bayern Munich since age 7
Matthias Ginter – with SC Freiburg since age 11
Benedikt Höwdes – with Schalke 04 since age 13
Per Mertesacker – with Hannover 96 since age 11

Continued on the following page

2014 WORLD CUP SQUAD *(FROM LEFT TO RIGHT)*
Julian Draxler – with Schalke 04 since age 8
Mario Götze – with Borussia Dortmund since age 9
Toni Kroos – with Hansa Rostock since age 12
Thomas Müller – with FC Bayern Munich since age 11
Bastian Schweinsteiger – with FC Bayern Munich since age 14
Christoph Kramer – with Bayer Leverkusen since age 8
Sami Khedira – with VfB Stuttgart since age 8
Mesut Özil – with RW Essen since age 12
Lukas Podolski – with 1. FC Cologne since age 10
Shkodran Mustafi – with Hamburger SV since age 15, then switched to Sampdoria Genoa via Everton; the only national team player who did not make an appearance in German Bundesliga
André Schürrle – with Mainz 05 since age 16
Miroslav Klose – the only world champion not to have trained at a youth performance center

For quality assurance, the DFB and the company Footpass must recertify the youth performance centers every three years. In doing so, the youth performance centers are evaluated in eight different areas: *strategy and finance, organization and operation, soccer instruction and evaluation, support and education, personnel, communication and cooperation, infrastructure and facilities, transparency and effectiveness*. Within their work with talent, the work of youth performance centers is divided into three age-dependent areas: elementary (up to age 11), advanced (ages 12-15), and performance (ages 16-18). The top talent is then prepared for the jump to a professional team during transition (ages 18-23), often by the club's B team or also on loan in order to gather experience in senior soccer.

"ONLY THOSE WHO REALLY HAVE THEIR HEAD TOGETHER MAKE IT TO THE TOP"

The young players need an education that prepares them for the sport after youth soccer. Mental training, therefore, plays a major role in youth performance centers. Hans-Dieter Hermann, DFB psychologist, says: "Only those who really have their head together make it to the top."[41] And it is not that easy. Sheltered in youth soccer, mistakes made without pressure from the media, fans, and spectators at out-of-town stadiums are not so harshly penalized yet. Of course, coaches demand maximum performance, but the players still get more time to develop. Since the mental preparation of young players is so critical, many clubs, meanwhile, work with mental conditioning coaches, particularly in youth soccer. Flattened hierarchies have, thus, become a thing of the past. As Matthias Sammer already said back in 2009: "Individualists, leading players, team players; they form a team hierarchy. We don't want leveling down!"[42]

"WE DON'T WANT LEVELLING DOWN"

Setting the course for the future

The youth performance centers became firmly established in Germany. It is now a part of the certification process for all 1st and 2nd Bundesliga clubs to operate a youth performance center that meets certain criteria (e.g. number of teams: mandatory is one team each from U12 to U19; listing the number of qualified coaches and staff, cooperation between schools and club, and much more). Clubs that do not meet these criteria cannot compete in the 1st and 2nd Bundesliga.

Dr. Jens Rehagel, director of the Hannover 96 performance center, is also impressed by this rapid development: "At the start of my tenure in 2005, the Bundesliga's youth performance centers moved and operated on very different levels. Over time, the clubs developed into commercial enterprises and their youth programs have grown accordingly and boarding schools have been established. Add to that the personnel, the psychological and educational staff, the full-time support, as well as the overall infrastructural requirements. These are all topics that in 2005, were still far off and the level has noticeably gone up in all areas." Head of the DFL, Christian Seifert, adds: "The introduction of youth performance centers was one of the Bundesliga's most important changes in direction. In doing so, we gained a two- to three-year advantage over international competitors."[43]

---

41 Quote from *ZEIT*. Available at: http://www.zeit.de/zeit-wissen/2006/03/Sportpsychologie.xml/seite-3.
42 Sammer, 2009, *ITK*. Available at: http://www.bdfl.de/trainerkongress/dokumentationen/2014-itk-2009.html.
43 See *Bild*. Available at: http://www.bild.de/sport/fussball/fussball-bundesligen/so-gut-sind-die-talent-schmieden-der-bundesliliga-35352394.bild.html.

"German players are exceptionally well trained."–
Arsène Wenger

The view has indeed changed. In the past, German clubs and associations looked longingly beyond their borders to find out what modern top-level training looked like; now clubs and associations from all over the world look to Germany to learn from the exemplary youth development and youth performance centers of the professional clubs. Recently, none other than Arsenal manager, Arsène Wenger, who has represented that club for 18 years, outed himself as a fan: "I love the way the Germans experience soccer. German players are exceptionally well trained; they have a good attitude; and simply possess all of the soccer attributes: witty playfulness and a fighting spirit."[44] It is no wonder, then, that three German world champions—Lukas Podolski, Per Mertesacker, and Mesut Özil—all appeared on Arsenal's roster at the beginning of the 2014-2015 season.

But England is also increasingly looking to German talent for their up-and-coming players. Gedion Zelalem (formerly of Hertha BSC), Serge Gnabry (VfB Stuttgart), and Thomas Eisfeld (BVB) have all been signed by Arsenal London. And they are not the only ones. Stephen Sama took the leap from Borussia Dortmund to FC Liverpool, and Samed Yesil went from Leverkusen to Anfield Road. Mainz goalkeeper Loris Karius received the fine-tuning of his soccer education at Manchester City and is now back in the English Premier League (Liverpool FC) as well as Ron-Robert Zieler who played during his youth a long time at Manchester United (now transferred to Leicester City FC). Richard Scudamore, head of the English Premier League since 1999, is delighted by the German talent. "These days, German clubs are producing some very fine soccer players. It is fun to watch the

---

44   Quoted in *Bundesliga*. Available at: http://www.bundesliga.de/de/wettbewerbe/champions-league/news/2013/verliebt-in-den-deutschen-fussball-arsene-wenger-fc-arsenal.php.

German talent in the Premier League. It is interesting that the Bundesliga reformed their youth development about ten years ago. We, too, want to develop star players again."[45]

But it is not just due to international scouting that England also focuses on German talent. An increase in international youth soccer competitions and games is leading to direct comparisons of performance levels on the club and association level. The DFB holds comparison games starting with the U15 national team. Players are scouted from all over Germany. The system of DFB bases and state-select soccer is helpful here. Subsequently, the junior national teams are comprised nearly exclusively of players from youth performance centers.

Increasing internationalization is also noticeable at the club level. The UEFA now operates a *youth league* for U19 teams as a parallel league to the Champions League. Starting with the 2015/2016 season, the respective U19 state champions will also be considered. The U19 teams of the respective professional teams play each other in the same groups and on the same days. The goal is high-quality competition and bringing youth players and pro teams closer together, since these teams frequently travel and are on the road together. Critics of this competition claim that the actual level of performance of the U19 teams isn't the determining criteria for participation. The *NextGen Series*, the precursor to the UEFA youth league, was financed by private investors and presented a similar high-quality model that was embraced by the European youth academies.

---

45   *Welt*. Available at: http://www.welt.de/newsticker/sport-news/article123356007/Premier-League-Chef-begeistert-von-deutschem-Fussball.html.

3.2 TRAINING AT VFB STUTTGART-TRADITION OBLIGES

VfB Stuttgart has a tradition of successful youth work. Currently more than 100 players who trained three or more years on youth teams are under contract nationally and internationally. Transfer proceeds from homegrown players are also significant. For instance, Mario Gomez transferred to FC Bayern Munich for the then record sum of over 30 million Euros, and the star midfielders Sami Khedira and Aleksandr Hleb also fetched huge sums, 14 million and 15 million Euros, respectively. Even the at the time of his transfer, inexperienced 20-year-old Bernd Leno brought the considerable sum of 8 million Euros.

From the VfB Stuttgart youth program: Sami Khedira

When VfB Stuttgart won the German national championship in 2007, they had more than seven home-trained players as part of their permanent personnel, including goalkeeper Timo Hildebrand; defenders Andreas Beck and Serdar Tasci; midfielders Christian Gentner and Sami Khedira; and forward Mario Gomez.

The term *young savages* made the rounds again and defined a generation that originated during the 2002/2003 season, when the VfB could celebrate a sensational second-place finish. Back then, players like Kevin Kuranyi, Christian Tiffert, Ioannis Amanatidis, and Andreas Hinkel, who played alongside experienced players like Zvonimir Soldo and Krassimir Balakov, drew attention with strong performances. The brand "young savages" became a seal of quality for the successful Stuttgart youth development program, which now is held in great esteem all over Europe. Sami Khedira played for Real Madrid in Spain and currently is under contract with the prestigious top Italian club Juventus Torino; Mario Gomez hunts goals for Besiktas Istanbul, Turkey, and Serdar Tasci plays at Spartak Moscow, Russia.

During the 2014/2014 season, Timo Baumgartl was the next player to step into the footsteps of the young savages around Timo Werner and company and continued the successful tradition on the professional team.

Physical therapy and weight room at the VfB Stuttgart

The successes of the junior A and B teams are further evidence of the long-term good and successful youth development work performed at VfB Stuttgart. With 10 junior A and 6 junior B championship titles, the VfB holds the record in youth titles, which shows that team successes in youth development do not play a minor part.

3.2.1 The newly constructed youth performance center– An important foundation for the future

The opening of the newly constructed youth performance center in November 2014 marked an investment in additional building blocks toward a continued leading role in youth development in the future. Here existing empirical evidence regarding infrastructure use and practicability in past years was used during the preliminary stages to push the infrastructural parameters and thereby the content quality of the Stuttgart youth performance center to a higher level yet again.

The youth complex is located right next to the professional wing, which results in close ties and interlocking through proximity and crossing paths. The features of the new structure even exceed the high licensing requirements for youth performance centers specified by the DFL. The new youth performance center offers VfB talent from U11 to U23 more than 250,000 square feet of floor space.

Next to locker rooms for each team it also contains fitness, weight, and recovery rooms and an office complex for the athletic director, coaches, scouts, psychologists, and the administration, thus creating a manpower conglomerate.

A photo gallery of players who grew up at VfB graces the walls and serves as a daily reminder to all players that the transition to pro soccer is deeply anchored in the club's philosophy.

Photo gallery of VfB Stuttgart players

In doing so, the club reacts to the constantly growing youth performance center structures at other professional clubs and meets the competition at the highest level.

"Youth development will remain a very important part of our strategy in the future. We have created an optimal infrastructure for our talent."

VfB Stuttgart president, Bernd Wahler

3.2.2 A conversation with Rainer Adrion, sports director at the youth performance center

Rainer Adrion has been the new sports director (U17 to U23) at the youth performance center since July 2014. He has lots of coaching experience in professional soccer, including working as assistant coach under Jogi Löw at VfB (1996-1998) and in the DFB's U21 youth soccer program, U23 coach at VfB, and worked with subsequent star players like Sami Khedira, Andreas Beck, Andreas Hinkel, Serdar Tasci, Mario Gomez, and others. He provides our readers with a general outline of the VfB's philosophy.

> **The most essential characteristics young players need to make it in the pro soccer business:**

"Talent is, of course, requisite and fundamental. The player should possess exceptional skills in a certain area. This can be, for instance, speed or coordination and technique. The more highly developed, the better. Coaches nurture, improve, and stabilize these skills and work specifically on weak points. A player's ongoing self-motivation to work on his weak areas and his strengths, his willingness to prevail against every type of obstacle, that is what matters in the end."

"ONE OF THE BUILDING BLOCKS IN OUR TRAINING IS CALLED WINNING MENTALITY"

> **Championship record holder as a training seal of approval:**

"We want to prepare players for professional soccer as best we can. One of the building blocks of this training is to develop the winning mentality that we demand from and nurture in every player, but also the team, every day. Of course, the training is more important than a title, but ideally the

VfB Stuttgart's new youth performance center

two should be combined. Titles are an affirmation of the work accomplished over the course of a year and a quality product of the club."

CREATING WORLD CHAMPIONS

The new youth performance center as a foundation for the future

"The new infrastructure allows us to improve the general conditions of our level of training, but the people who give life to these improved structures are what make the difference. The compactness of this new complex facilitates the principle of short distances and intensive communication.

The offices where coaches, scouts, administrative staff, and athletic directors work together every day on improvements and optimization are located on one level.

Experts from the individual areas ensure a comprehensive education:

Physical therapists for prophylactic improvement and individual guidance and care of talent, and with respect to regeneration.

The psychologist as constant contact person and advisor to players, coaches, and individual teams.

The athletic trainers who work with the players on the field or in the new weight room.

The physicians who care for injured or sick players.

The coaching teams for the performance teams consist of a full-time head coach, a part-time assistant coach, a full-time goalkeeping coach, and the previously mentioned athletic trainers, who are also full-time staff members.

The close interlocking of the individual areas and the principle of short distances create additional free time within the players' busy daily schedule.

Our close cooperation with elite soccer schools has allowed us to considerably improve the volume and frequency and, thereby, the quality of training units.

We would like our players not to take our new infrastructure for granted, but rather consider it a privilege. This requires a good measure of humility and respect toward all staff, from the laundress to the own team members. That is also an important part of our players' personal development. To highlight this, we have established a behavior ABC that is mandatory for every player.

Many of the day-to-day details are also governed in this ABC (e.g., choosing a physician, and also the use of social media and cell phones), which can be considered a kind of code of behavior for VfB players. Next to certain values (e.g., greeting all staff and teammates, punctuality, orderliness, respectful interaction), outward appearance is also regulated."

Youth academy at the stadium:
"The view into the stadium from the rooms is meant to inspire additional motivation to pursue one's goal of becoming a pro soccer players at VfB."

Gym:
"The view from the weight room onto the training grounds at the youth performance center was also deliberately chosen to internalize training goals and reinforce personal goals."

Levels of communication

"We consider the newly constructed dining hall another building block of cooperative life at our club. Pro players, coaches, youth players, and club staff meet for lunch in a separate area, eat sport-appropriate meals together, and swap ideas. This contributes to team spirit within our club and further identification.

We see the soccer tennis field that was built between the professional wing and the youth locker room wing as an additional meeting place for all players, where young and old meets and plays and has fun together in a casual atmosphere."

3.3 THE KROOS FAMILY– A DOWN-HOME SUCCESS STORY

An important pillar of the German national team: Toni Kroos

In spite of difficult conditions at Hansa Rostock, the U19 team is an integral part of the Bundesliga North. This is due in no small part to Roland Kroos, who coached the U19 team for many years and is now in charge of the U23. As a blatant outsider he was able to lead his team all the way to the German national championship final in the 2011/2012 season, and in doing so, eliminated Bayern Munich during the semi-

Two succesful soccer pros, Toni and Felix Kroos

finals. In the final, his U19 team narrowly lost to VfL Wolfsburg in extra time. With the beginning of the 2015/2016 season, Kroos now coaches the Hansa Rostock U23 team.

But Roland Kroos is not just a coach but also the father of two sons who both became professional soccer players. Felix plays for 1. FC Union Berlin and Toni became world champion in 2014 and plays for Real Madrid.

3.3.1   Interview with Roland Kroos

> Although the commercial opportunities at Hansa Rostock are very limited, the U19 always manages to bring outstanding results. What is your formula for success?

"In our daily work, as coaches we, of course, strive to make the most of our opportunities. We do so by, on the one hand, working on the strengths and weaknesses of individual players and, on the other hand, by promoting team unity so our strengths as a unit can unfold. That is the prerequisite to surviving in the A Youth Bundesliga which is not a given for a team like Hansa Rostock."

> Your location is a definite disadvantage for attracting talent as compared to other professional youth performance centers. What methods and options do you use to that end?

"Mecklenburg-Vorpommern is a large state, but in past years the quality of training in the smaller clubs has continued to go down. Still, we put enormous effort into sighting players. We do a lot of scouting trips with our coaches to acquire suitable players for Hansa Rostock, but due to the competitive situation, it has become considerably more difficult to win talent over to our way. Other clubs have more manpower due to their commercial opportunities, and that, of course, also extends to their scouting. We have learned to work with it and make the best of our situation."

"BOTH HAD ENTHUSIASM AND JOY FOR LEARNING"

> Both of your sons, Felix and Toni, became pros. You coached both of them as club coach. When did you first foresee their developmental trajectory?

"Since childhood, both have been clearly better in their class than their teammates and opponents, and both had talent. Toni was the more talented of the two. But talent is only the basis. Nurturing it was the key so they could continue to develop in the best possible way."

> You did additional training with your boys. What did that training look like, and how important was that individual training for their continued journey?

"Even as children, both were already crazy about soccer, and we played a lot with family and friends at the park or in the backyard.

Beyond that we worked primarily on technique: playing with both feet and technical movement sequences. Details were automated. For example, I made sure that the ball was not just settled but was controlled in an open body position to create a consecutive situation. The prerequisite was enthusiasm and joy for learning, which both had. And then there were the competitive successes. That confirmed their progress."

> Toni went from Hansa Rostock to FC Bayern. That was a big step. Were there other offers, and why did he go straight to one of the biggest clubs in the world?

"Of course we talked about it as a family, but in the end it was Toni's decision, and that meant joining FC Bayern. Of importance was that during their conversations the team's decision-makers presented him with a clear athletic path. He saw it as an opportunity and took it. He went to boarding school at Bayern, and there was a feel-good factor right from the start with the people who attended to him there and the entire environment. That made a quick integration into the athletic realm easier. There he also developed confidence in his own performance and thereby quickly gained recognition on the field during professional training at the highest level."

> Then came Leverkusen as an interim step.

"That loan was important for his continued athletic career. There he got the opportunity to play regularly, had a different standing, was immediately a key player, and returned to Munich stronger and more mature."

> Felix switched to Werder Bremen and is now a regular player in the Bundesliga.

"He recently started to play defensive center midfield, and his technical training serves him well in this position. But due to the current situation [fall of the 2014/2015 season] in Bremen with the relegation struggle, the play against the ball is bolder. But this is also an important learning process in his development. Regardless of the position, it is important that he has regular appearances and thereby achieves continuity. The rest will come."

> Since the summer of 2014, Toni has been playing for Real Madrid. This club has an incredible charisma worldwide, but particularly in Spain, were the players are revered as superstars. Is that a valuable experience for your son?

"During my visit to Madrid I was able to experience this firsthand. It is one of the biggest clubs in the world and consequently has a presence at every street corner, especially in the media.

But Toni has never let the hype or the extremely negative news, as well as the headline superlatives, affect him. It is not consistent with his character. He can handle it, and his groundedness and self-perception and relativization of things help him there. He is focused on his performance and that speaks for itself."

> The media coined him the "interior designer" in midfield. Can you explain that term?

"As a child, he was one of the smallest ones and had to intuitively find solutions for himself to stand his ground against the bigger kids, and thus avoid direct tackles. One of his greatest strengths in training was anticipating plays. Who gets open in the spaces, how much time do I have in possession—and thereby quickly grasps the right decision. He has acquired and cemented the ability to anticipate two to three moves in advance. This playing intelligence has been refined over the years under better and better conditions, and the higher possession at Real Madrid with him in midfield are proof of that."

> As a father, how do you handle all that excitement in the soccer business?

"I can't and don't want to influence it, but it is important to keep it all in perspective. I follow my sons' games as a coach, and when we talk on the phone and exchange views there are no major analyses but rather I am a father first. Toni and Felix were raised to be independent, have learned to handle the business, and it is important that they make their own experiences. Of course in doing so, mistakes happen, but important lessons are learned in the process."

Kroos playing in Madrid's Starting Eleven

> With your experience as coach and father, what is your advice to parents of talented players? How can parents best support their child?

"As parents we should support our child as best we can and show him that you cannot rely on talent alone. That it requires sacrifice, meaning that in order to progress you have to severely limit your free time. And a young player experiences lows where an intact family and mutual trust become very important. It is good to find a healthy medium of praise but also constructive criticism. Money should remain in the background because it is more important to find a club with good and competent coaches. It can be a smaller club for taking the next valuable step. External influences should be cushioned by the family, and humility and groundedness are important counselors on the way there."

3.4 THE BERLIN WAY– TRAINING TOP TALENT FOR PRO SOCCER

3.4.1 Introduction

Like all other Bundesliga teams, Hertha BSC's goal is to prepare their own young talent for their professional team. This is not only based on a firm conviction but has become a matter of tradition. The Boateng brothers, Ashkan Dejagah, Patrick Ebert, Sejad Salihovic, or currently John Brooks and Nico Schulz are just a few names from a training tradition of top talent for pro soccer. Of course, the club takes particular pride in the fact that Boateng is one of the players who became world champions in Rio in 2014. The degree to which Hertha Berlin values their youth development is evident in this remark by the athletic manager, Michael Preetz: "At Hertha BSC it is a must to rely on our own talent and to help them make it."[46]

Jerome Boateng (left), Patrick Ebert (top center), Kevin-Prince Boateng (center bottom), Ashkan Dejagah (right)

---

46 *Kicker.* Available at: http://www.kicker.de/news/fussball/bundesliga/startseite/589855/artikel_preetz_hertha-muss-auf-die-eigenen-talente-setzen.html.

3.4.2   Frank Vogel talks

Frank Vogel

Since 2003, Frank Vogel has been the athletic director of the soccer academy and has been a part of the development of top talent. He now explains the way things are currently done in Berlin to get new top talent to fill those shoes.

"Hertha Berlin's good long-term youth development work is not only evident in the number of current Bundesliga players who trained in Berlin, but the certification performed by the DFB, DFL, and Footpass attests to the youth performance center's top level. At the last certification Berlin was awarded the highest distinction (three stars). There were always positive changes in the scoring of the individual evaluated areas. Effectiveness with respect to club affinity and transition to pro soccer remain at the highest level.

02 Soccer academy vision for training

Excerpt from the Hertha BSC's doctrine

Our long-term commitment and corresponding intensive support resulted in a better than 75% effectiveness rating of the academy in past certification cycles. That makes us proud and speaks to our long-term philosophy.

Hany Mukhtar, Marius Gersbeck (both European champions with the U19 national team), John Anthony Brooks, Änis Ben-Hatira, and Nico Schulz are current examples of permeability because they were trained in our own youth program. And all of the players listed were born in Berlin.

For talent selection, we focus primarily on the Berlin Market whose population density and number of training facilities provide a great breadth of players. By doing so, we promote and increase affinity with Hertha BSC in the city and within our club. With few exceptions, all players on the U17, U19, and U23 teams are born in Berlin.

Due to today's transparent market and the battle for talent in competition with other clubs, we have also chosen this path for its cost effectiveness and the associated manpower in order to offer our Berlin talent a top-level home in Berlin. This has the advantage that the players don't have to fit into a new social hierarchy. They grow up within the safety and comfort of their families while simultaneously enjoying the benefits of intensive talent development at Hertha BSC.

The demands of today's top-level soccer are high. They include great momentum, great playing ability and ball control in tight spaces and at top speed, as well as a confident, performance-oriented mindset. Players must be optimally prepared for this during the phases of training.

To fill these building blocks with additional content, the U17, U19, and U23 coaches in coordination with the professional coaches determine the club's currently best talent for the "project top talent". These players receive specific and more detailed support to prepare even better for the demands of pro soccer.

On the one hand, we show our top talent a clear path to Hertha BSC's professional team. On the other hand, we also incite and motivate those players who are currently not participating in that special building block to also achieve that goal. As a result, the players who are already a part of the talent group must continuously hold their ground and can't drop off. Performance is always rewarded, which is why every player has a chance.

With regard to the talented, up-and-coming players who are supposed to be admitted to the professional team, the transition from youth or amateur soccer to the pros is especially critical. Since young players have age-specific deficiencies and performance fluctuations in the different areas of their performance, it is important that additional coaches who are specially qualified for this task based on a detailed strength and weakness analysis work one-on-one with these young players. There is major support for this particularly because young players in their ascent to the professional team are subject to countless changes and influences. At the same time, coordination between U19 and U23 and the pros is important because the switch between the different teams creates technical, tactical, and especially mental and physical challenges.

Every 14 days, a talent development training session for the top talent group takes place under the direction of the pro soccer department's assistant coach. They receive separate training in action speed, settling and controlling the ball, passing accuracy, and tactical sequences. The demands of pro soccer are, of course, on a different level than those of youth soccer. Ideally, the professional coaches transfer sequences from pro soccer to the top talent.

Moreover, this regular support reduces the adjustment difficulties of switching to a professional team. All of this is subject to supervision by the head coach. He also takes a regular look at U19 and U23 players to get a detailed overview of the current level of performance. He regularly adds individual top talent to professional training sessions. The close communication and interlocking with the professional realm ensures that every top talent has the opportunity to prove himself at the highest level and gets a chance to take the leap to the very top. The close link between youth and professional departments ensures that every top talent receives the best possible individual support and attention on his path.

Players must get used to the increased demands on the older teams or rather professional teams. But they can also experience firsthand the quality that exists there. They learn the differences in all areas and sometimes are even surprised at the definite difference in quality from youth soccer. This also results in a realistic self-assessment of their own performance capacity and in an even more specific and detailed analysis of the things that need improving.

Participating in training units with the pros is another step here. To prevail is a process. In conversation with the boys, we notice that it is a very big step. Attempts at shrinking the big gap between youth and professional soccer are beginning to come to fruition. Due to the previously mentioned measures, quicker integration of young players into the professional team and long-term improvement of playing quality in general are clearly apparent.

TRAINING SCHEDULE
HERTHA BSC U19 (2014/2015)
Top Talent

DAY	DATE	START	CONTENT
Mon		5:30pm	**Video analysis of last game**
		6pm	**Practice:** Regeneration or game replacement workout
Tues		9:30am	**Special training at school:** Coordination and stabilization based on individual plan or FMS results or technique training like passing, crossing, pendulum training based on strength/ weakness profile (low exertion/mandatory school period)
Wed		9:30am	**Special training at school:** Individual and group tactics such as tackling practice, switching play in small groups, actively scoring and preventing goals, position-specific sequences, or strength and power training
		5:30pm	**Team or talent training** with assistant coach 1st team: Every two weeks with emphasis on passing, ball manipulation, feints at top speed as well as tackles and forms of play up to 6-on-6 max., also from a tactical point of view, opening the game and passing into the end zone
Thurs		9:30am	**Special training at school:** Alternative sports like gymnastics (martial arts in preparation) or coordination and stabilization
		4:30pm	**Individual video coaching of a current player:** Once a month with the athletic director; day is flexible
		5:30pm	**Team training**
Fri		4:45pm	**Team training**
Sat		11:45am	**Meeting**
		1pm	**League game**
Sun			Day off: Since fixtures vary, the team's order of events for Sunday to Tuesday is flexible

Illustration: A talent's week

We have created definite guidelines and content for development. Our constant communication, also with the professionals, allows us to continuously challenge ourselves to coordinate, implement, and enhance potential improvements for individual support. This close interweaving is essential to our doctrine.

Close communication is the foundation

Every Monday, the coaches, youth performance center director, teachers, physical therapists, and fitness trainers meet to analyze, discuss, and evaluate general training and playing issues, as well as an update on the talent's recorded training content and current development.

Hertha BSC cooperates with two elite soccer and sports schools. This affiliation is considered particularly important and necessary as it ensures up to three additional training units in the morning. The club makes special allowances for exams. On the other hand, absences for games or selection proceedings are easier to organize, and missed work can be made up. In our doctrine, the school is a mainstay and a priority because not every player makes it to the pros and, therefore, must have another leg to stand on. School is learning training and should have an effect on adolescents in terms of soccer development for as long as possible. And as a club we also have a social responsibility.

About individual video coaching

All select team games are recorded. Of course, the coach also uses these videos to analyze the technical–tactical behavior of the entire team. But the videos also give us the opportunity for individual support. Different scenes from the game are discussed individually with the player. The intent is to show the player critical scenes and also to communicate about perception, learning, and implementation of soccer content through positive guidance. Often an exchange about the perception of a game situation is important in order to understand the player's behavior during a certain moment. This additional coaching is also meant to make the player aware of the importance of his path to the club.

A sports scientist who is also a psychologist then takes another separate look at the top talent and analyzes his observations with the individual players.

The focus here is cognition of game situations, body language, and actions in certain situations.

In addition to the annual sports medicine examination required by the DFL, a muscle function analysis is done of all the clubs' top talent. The appropriate treatments or training programs are then individually designed based on the results.

All of this ensures the highest level of support. Of particular importance is the continued development within the training process as opposed to the momentary performance. The permanent support—also in reflection and joint analysis—the customized training content, and, of course, the close communication between the various areas are intended to meet the requirements of a complete education. This also includes workshops like anti-violence training and media training as permanent parts of instruction. "In order to meet our ambitious goals we need an organizational structure that truly lives up to our integrative approach."

The listed daily demands generate a lot of stress for a talent. The club, therefore, tries to control the stressful stimuli through purposeful time management. To achieve an optimal relationship between recovery and exertion, the recorded content of training units and the lists of participants are used as a control mechanism. In addition, the top talent have the opportunity for privacy at the boarding school. There they receive a sport-appropriate diet, can retreat to the privacy of their rooms (sleep and rest), and have access to recreational activities like Ping-Pong and PlayStation. Youth director Frank Vogel lists the causes of stress for Hertha talent: "The DFB or state selection process as well as the players' commute within the Berlin metropolis are a source of major mental and physical stress that must be managed in order to avoid injuries and mental fatigue."

Outlook: Another building block in the works

"For years we have made the case for this, and the project is finally being realized." In summer 2015, the elite soccer academy will be constructed on club grounds, which will bring important relief in terms of time and space to accommodate the high level of intensity of school and youth performance soccer. The responsible parties hope that the close linkage and integration between soccer and academic instruction will facilitate a push forward into a new dimension of holistic talent development.

Organizational Strukure
Hertha BSC Soccer Academy

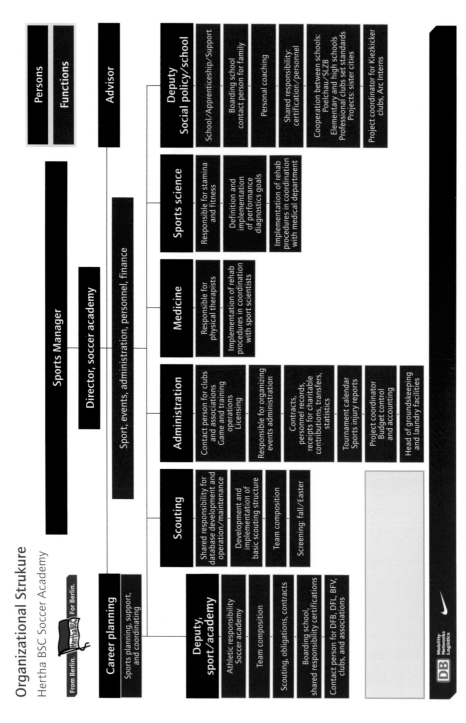

Organizational structure at the Berlin youth development center

3.5 SCHOOL, CHELSEA, AND THE FIGHT FOR THE DREAM– MAURICE NEUBAUER OF U19 OF FC SCHALKE 04

When Maurice Neubauer gets up at 6:45 on Monday mornings, he embarks on a completely normal daily routine. At 7:20am, the shuttle service of his club FC Schalke picks him up to get him to school on time. Maurice attends an elite soccer academy and is about to graduate with a technical diploma. Along with the other soccer players in his class who play for youth teams at Borussia Dortmund, Rot-Weiß Hessen, and Fortuna Düsseldorf, there are also normal (i.e., non-soccer players) students in his class.

After a sport-appropriate buffet lunch for all students, he has classes until 3:50pm, "We soccer players have access to a leisure room where we can spend the time until soccer practice under the supervision of a guidance counselor. Here we can do our homework or relax before practice." The walk to the Schalke grounds takes only three minutes, and the Schalke players make their way to the field. From 5:30pm on, the Schalke U19 team requires Maurice's absolute concentration during the training unit.

For years, FC Schalke 04 has been playing for the Bundesliga West U19 title, and there is lots of competition within the team. Players have to prove themselves every day. After practice, Maurice is dropped off at home along with other players who live farther away. "It normally takes 30 minutes to get to my hometown of Recklinghausen. I live with my parents and get home around 9pm. Then I eat dinner and get some rest so I can be fit again for the next day," says Maurice.

He gladly accepts that fulfilling his dream requires sacrifice. "My goal is to become a professional soccer player, and I want to make it as far as possible. To do that, I have to put other things aside. That's the way it is." While he has a steady girlfriend of two years and his buddies at home, he does not get to see any of them very often.

"MY BUDDIES PARTY AT THE DISCO. I PARTY, TOO, ON THE FIELD."

"When I have some free time, I do something with her or spend time with my friends, but I need my regimented life and can't just go bar hopping, or I won't be able to perform. My buddies go to the disco, and I rest. Sometimes I would like to join them, but I can party on the soccer field."

Maurice has already learned the hard way that the road to his goal can get quite bumpy. Although he has moved up through Schalke 04's youth teams since 2004, he was rejected after the U15. "The coach at that time told me that I didn't have it anymore and had to leave the club. Of course, I was quite sad. Back then my world just caved in." He switched to the MSV Duisburg U16 and fought his way back. After a year of good performances, the responsible parties invited him back to the *Knappen* (Miners, the team of Schalke). "In retrospect, athletically it was a definite step backwards, but I was able to progress and came back stronger. Schalke is my favorite club. I have been a fan since earliest childhood and attended their games with my parents. I was so happy to be back."

In the UEFA youth league, U19 players make their first international experiences (here Felix Platte in a game against FC Chelsea London)

Maurice plays in the left-back position and is currently one of the team's permanent members. As of last season, the U19 also competes internationally in the youth league established by UEFA. Since then they have already dueled with big names like FC Chelsea and FC Barcelona, who they narrowly lost to during last year's semi-finals.

"These games are an absolute highlight, and the level of play is quite a bit higher than the nationals. There is less time and space, and every mistake is punished mercilessly." The U19 team gets to travel to international games on the same plane as the pros. "We get to meet one or the other pro, exchange ideas and take away quite a bit." There is respect and pride in his voice.

After their own games, the U19'ers watch the Champions League matches of the Schalke 04 pros. "That's always something special. I sat in the stadium at Stamford Bridge and rooted for them." He paid particular attention to the players who played in the full-back position. "I don't have a specific role model, but I think Ivanovic of Chelsea is amazing. I can learn a lot from him."

Of course, he has to make up the work he missed during his travels. "Our school offers tutoring, which I take advantage of. I really want to graduate and for that I need to apply myself."

His family fully supports him. "My parents have come to every game since I was little. Back then they always drove me to practice as well." Even though his father has also played at a high level in the past, he hangs back during the post-game analyses. "When we win, he is happy for us; when we lose, he comforts me. But we don't talk about individual situations from the game. That's my coach's job. During my first U19 season I did not play in the beginning. Then I worked every day on the weaknesses the coach discussed with me. His criticism helped me, I got better and earned a permanent spot."

The next step is the U23 at Schalke 04. "To me all that matters is the next step, and that's the next practice. To move up I have to improve in all areas."

That is still a long way off, and it would be a small dream come true for Maurice if he were allowed to train with the pros sometime. And what happens if he doesn't make it to the pros? "I want to lay a foundation with my technical diploma, and if it doesn't happen for me, I will definitely still work in the sports field."

But to raise the likelihood that it will happen, he plans to "work hard and fight every single day."

3.6 VFL WOLFSBURG– HOLISTIC THINKING AS THE KEY TO YOUTH DEVELOPMENT

Youth development at VfL Wolfsburg's youth performance center is essentially based on three pillars: **soccer training, character development, and educational training**. Experts and professionals look after the Bundesliga stars of tomorrow in all areas and try to ensure the best possible support in these respective areas.

One crucial point that, to some extent, is also determined by the character of the individual players is educational training. Each year, more than 400 talented young players are trained in the 1st and 2nd Bundesliga's 36 youth performance centers alone. It is understandable that not all of them make the jump to the very top of professional soccer. It is, therefore, the club's special responsibility to prepare these players for a "second" career so that these young people are equipped for life and the possibility of a subsequent working life outside of professional soccer. Moreover, experience shows that those who persevere in the end are primarily the ones who stay in school and graduate. In that case, a large portion of the personal development can be attributed to parallel demands of school, education, and soccer.

Self-reliance, independence, and self-organization are skills the young players must possess. Says Fabian Wohlgemuth, director of the VfL Wolfsburg's youth performance center: "In the past, there have frequently been players who along with their parents thought that it would be better to focus exclusively on soccer. In cases like this we usually discourage that approach because we consider it our duty to produce not only well-trained soccer players, but also grounded individuals with prospects outside of the sport. In fact, there is empirical evidence that most of the players that focused 'exclusively' on soccer in the end were unable to make the jump to paid soccer."

Those who are able to optimally manage all of these areas when they are young are also stable enough to bear up against the stress and pressure of pro soccer. But anyone not disciplined enough to finish school or career training also lacks the character traits and necessary self-discipline to make it to the top.

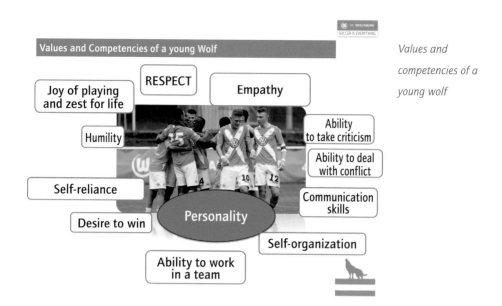

Values and competencies of a young wolf

The director of the Wolfsburg youth performance center likes to use home-grown talent Maximilian Arnold and Robin Knoche, who today are starting players on the pro team, as examples: "The ascent of Knoche and Arnold has provided an interesting insight for us. Why the two of them, and not five or six others? The answer: Knoche and Arnold are intelligent, always have been cognizant of the qualifications they acquired at VfL Wolfsburg to successfully straddle the divide of academic demands as high school seniors and professional soccer training. Knoche and Arnold were very good students during the first half of the day, gratefully accepting all kinds of support at the boarding school, and in doing so learned that accepting help makes things much easier. And watching them on the soccer field, it was apparent: Knoche and Arnold never selfishly cultivated their strengths, but rather always remembered what they needed to work on every day. Someone who makes himself comfortable, who considers our careful support a convenience, will never reach the point of playing in 50 Bundesliga games."[47]

At the VfL Wolfsburg youth performance center where Maximilian Arnold and Robin Knoche, as well as Julian Brandt (now at Bayer Leverkusen), Sebastian Polter (now at Queens Park Rangers), Florian Hartherz (now Paderborn), Tolga Cigerci (now Hertha BSC), Sebastian Stolze, and Paul Seguin completed their soccer development, the players

---

47   Quote from N. interview *Dfb.de*. Available at: http://www.dfb.de/news/detail/wohlgemuth-wolfsburgs-anspruch-spiel-zu-dominieren-58765/p/2/.

benefitted from the close proximity to the partner school. Eichendorffschule is less than five minutes walking distance.

Learning support for players at the youth performance center is a fundamental part of VfL Wolfsburg's education concept. With all the focus on performance soccer, personal development in general and schooling and career training in particular are considered very important here.

Youth performance center director Fabian Wohlgemuth emphasizes: "During the development of a young player, and especially during the transition to men's soccer, it is the little things that count. We believe that alert and receptive players better meet the complex demands of modern soccer. We are happy to have Eicheldorffschule as a cooperative partner who addresses the wants and needs of our players. It is extremely important for our youth to graduate so they are able to continue their development outside of soccer. There are a number of good reasons for this. From a sports perspective it can be assumed that a player can only give his best performance when he is able to fully concentrate on training and competing without being burdened by problems of everyday life."

In this context, school can be a major source of conflict that must be counteracted from the start. All participants must continuously focus on academic performance and social skills to be able to not only support athletic development, but also to meet the overall responsibility for the young people in care, because life during and after a soccer career always matters. This philosophy is shared by all who participate in the development of these young people and is the basis for all educational activity at VfL Wolfsburg's youth performance center.

Cooperative efforts with Eichendorffschule are supported by a regional team. The regional team consists of club representatives (director, athletic director, educators, coaches, representatives from the girls VfL youth department), school representatives (high school administration, high school representatives and coordinators, girls program coordinators), representatives of the Lower Saxony Soccer Association (base camp coordinator, person in charge of school soccer), as well as city or state representatives. The DFB provides a 30,000 Euro annual budget for the cooperation of elite soccer academies. This budget can increase if the women's youth department is also incorporated, as is the case at VfL Wolfsburg. The regional team representatives, who are led by a speaker, then decide in joint sessions how the money will be used. The DFB stipulates that spending must be project-linked for the purpose of cooperation between elite soccer academies and the club's youth department.

Wohlgemuth, who, in his capacity as youth performance center director, is himself a member of the regional team, explains: "The regional team, on the one hand, serves as a communication platform for joint discussion of issues of cooperation among representatives of school, club, and also the Lower Saxony Soccer Association. On the other hand, it is a way to set the course for working cooperation between VfL and the school or possibly fine-tune the same."

Within the scope of this structure, VfL Wolfsburg also holds an annual teacher conference, where teachers and coaches for the respective age groups meet and discuss academic standing of the respective players. In this regard, communication between school and sport is very close so that immediate action can usually be taken with respect to academic performance or problems. A player may have to forgo training if his academic performance has dropped too much or he is in danger of not graduating.

VfL Wolfsburg's boarding school houses 26 players, ages U14 to U19. A team of five educators looks after the players around the clock. The youth performance center director explains: "Over the years, we have devised a good system to guide our players and educational coaches. It is important that we offer a professional environment while also creating a family atmosphere that nurtures our players in their development. Only those who feel at ease, who trust us, are able to bridge the divide of school and soccer and continue to progress. Our educators help with that."[48]

---

48   Quote from *dfb.de*. Available at: http://www.dfb.de/news/detail/wohlgemuth-wolfsburgs-anspruch-spiel-zu-dominieren-58765/.

*"WE PROVIDE BOTH A PROFESSIONAL LEARNING ENVIRONMENT
AND A FAMILY ATMOSPHERE"*

Our players get as much support as possible on a daily basis. Homework tutoring and academic support *(study time)* takes place every afternoon at the boarding school and includes homework, test and exam prep, basic assistance, revision or make-up of content deficiencies, all the way to tutoring, official errands, and also help with everyday problems—all are mitigated in the best way possible. External students not residing at the boarding school are also able to work with the teachers or to secure their continued development after school through links to several cooperation partners in line with their soccer training.

Fabian Wohlgemuth explains: "Our teachers support our players in every way. They always have a sympathetic ear and provide the players with the necessary support in everyday life." In doing so, regular contact with the relevant parties (teachers, training supervisor) is essential. How much value the parents of young players today place on schooling can also be deduced from the fact that much importance is attached to choice of club and quality and linkage of academic and professional training.[49]

"It is becoming increasingly apparent that farsighted parents consider schooling a definite part of holistic youth development. Our concept has been convincing here as well. In Wolfsburg, academic and athletic success can be reconciled," says Wohlgemuth. The VfL Wolfsburg boarding school has a rule: Anyone not in school or career training has to move out. There is also close communication between teachers and coaches. When a player's school performance drops, he has to forgo soccer training so he can internalize the academic content. Performance evaluation talks for each player between U10 and U19 are held at least twice a year. During these conversations, the coach issues the player a brief evaluation and points out the areas in which he expects to see improvement. These talks always include academic performance.

---

49 *Sport Bild*, 2015, Available at: http://www.genios.de/presse-archiv/artikel/SBIL/20150204/der-brutale-kampf-um-talente/131648960.html.

"DEMANDS ON THE PROS OF TOMORROW ARE RAPIDLY INCREASING"

Coaches also attach a lot of importance to a solid academic performance, because an alert and bright mind is generally more receptive at training.

In addition, the teachers at VfL Wolfsburg offer behavioral training as needed, such as coaching for learning, concentration, job application, and social skills, in order to provide the young talent with guidance and support in their daily lives.

The challenges for the professional soccer players of tomorrow have increased enormously. Dealing with the media, the daily press, social media, and especially the everyday challenges of fans, family, and the team due to professional competition creates a huge amount of pressure resulting from expectations that some young players are unable to cope with at first. Meanwhile, many youth performance centers, like VfL Wolfsburg, work with sport psychologists and mental coaches to prepare the up-and-coming players as much as possible for these challenges.

Fabian Wohlgemuth underscores the importance of this collaboration: "Demands on the pros of tomorrow are rapidly increasing. In addition to huge expectations, the players must be able to handle small setbacks. One of the goals of working with the mental coach is developing the ability of conscious problem management and identifying strategies that result in an optimal performance. Next to the excellent work of our team coaches, this provides additional support to better bring forth the individual character of each player." The VfL Juniors are prepared for the mental challenges as well as coping with stressful situations within the scope of this collaboration. Offers are also created for the coaches of the youth teams so they are able to prepare the players even better for competition and to better guide them based on their individual personalities.

The situations are reflected on, analyzed, and evaluated in private conversations, especially after personal setbacks (injury, athletic performance crisis, personal problems), before possible solutions and reactions are searched for. The work of the mental coach affects the entire training. At VfL Wolfsburg, basic elements of personal development that the players can draw on later in their soccer career are already developed at the U10 level. With the U10 players, this is done through simple Qigong exercises before and after practice where players learn to strictly focus on and control their breathing. A major increase in the players' ability to concentrate was detected after just a short time.

In the area of performance, elements of character are sometimes trained with a large group. For instance, with scenario-based training where play is 10-on-7, the outnumbered team must successfully defend a 2-0 lead for 10 minutes, or case-based training where penalty shots must be executed as realistically as possible in the training process.

With regard to the purpose of these training methods, youth performance center director Fabian Wohlgemuth says: "In close games at the highest level, a team's success and failure are often determined by mindset. By practicing scenarios or by learning special concentration techniques we try to provide the students with a winner's mentality that will become an attribute down the road."

The work of a youth performance center closely links all three pillars: **soccer training, character development, and educational training**. They interact and depend on each other when it comes to a talent making it all way to the top.

VfL Wolfsburg U19 team during the 2011/2012 season

3.7 INTERVIEW WITH WERNER MICKLER, DFB PSYCHOLOGIST

Until 1996, Werner Mickler worked at the Institute of Psychology at the German Sport University Cologne before going into business for himself. As head of the sport psychology focus area he is a lecturer in the soccer instructor training program at DFB Hennef and supports different professional teams and coaches. He also works with the Rhineland Olympic Center, the German Taekwondo Association, and other sport entities.

> There are people who expect a sport psychologist to perform "magic," while others completely undervalue this important work. Is there a healthy middle ground within these points of view?

"The sport psychologist is an expert in a certain area, just like a fitness trainer or a physical therapist meets his respective responsibilities in soccer and, thus, has a support function within the complex sport that is soccer.

A starting point in working with the athletes that is particularly important in youth soccer is to provide them with the tools to master certain situations. On the other hand, being there for the coaches ("coach to coach"), helping them approach certain situations, and giving them the tools to do so. The question is whether or not the sport psychologist has the qualifications to perform and meet both obligations.

"CHILDREN AND ADOLESCENTS SHOULD HAVE FUN WINNING AND NOT BE TRAINED TO FEAR LOSING"

There is no magic or hocus pocus, but rather a professional approach, which means systematic, deliberate psychological training to learn certain things and to practice and apply them."

> Many clubs already focus primarily on winning in children's soccer. Is that the right path to personal development?

"It is about striking a healthy balance. Children and adolescents should have fun winning and not be trained to fear losing. The emotional component plays an important role here.

The younger the players, the more emphasis should be placed on fun, and the absolute desire to win as a performance parameter should only become a priority as they approach adult soccer. The coaches and responsible parties in a club should ask themselves: Why do players begin to play soccer? Because they want to have fun! This emotional component must be nurtured because it develops and shapes the character. Then I am ready to learn new things, and that works better and faster with positive emotions. And this sense of fun should be maintained into adult soccer and beyond."

> **Why is it so important to provide the young players access to psychologists at the youth performance centers?**

"In my opinion they should be sport psychologists, meaning experts who are familiar with athletes and the challenges they will face, in order to provide professional advice. For instance, when specific nutritional questions or other things come up, advice should be sought from external professionals who can handle these matters externally. In the forefront is the athletic development of the talent, and topics such as time management, solving stressful situations, and stress resistance should already be taught rudimentarily in youth performance centers so the athlete is prepared when he moves up to adult soccer. At that point, hardly any coach will take time for that, which is why this should also be handled in accordance with the respective club's philosophy."

> **A lot of young players dream of a soccer career, but very few reach their goal. To what extent is the psychologist required?**

"Of course every player should be trained so he can play at the highest level possible. But it is a very difficult road to the top. For that reason, the players and the people surrounding them, especially the family, must be made aware that in the end only very few are able to reach that goal.

"OFTEN THERE ARE OBSTACLES OR SETBACKS ONE MUST LEARN TO HANDLE"

That is why major emphasis should be placed on the dual career, on continued academic advancement, to have a second leg to stand on. Not only do performance fluctuations occur, but in performance sports there is always a risk of injury, and the player, and also the parents, must be made aware of this.

In some cases, it is important to devise intermediate goals so the player doesn't go straight to the top but plays on an amateur team or a U23 team first. This intermediate step should not be viewed as a step backwards but as progress, because many times there are obstacles or setbacks one must learn to handle. What matters is to protect the player from constant overloading. Here a different coach can also set new impulses because he has a different perspective."

> Some youth performance centers also offer media training. Is it possible to reenact a real situation par for par later in pro soccer?

Leroy Sané: Even as a young pro the requirements for dealing with the public are numerous.

"A real situation can never be reenacted par for par. We are unable to do so, and it is not possible in other areas either. We want to make sure they learn to react to certain situations with certain questions and interviewing techniques and in doing so, provide them with certain strategies they can employ in a difficult situation. How do I comment on certain things, and how do I react to uncomfortable questions? The question is this: Is the player able to handle the tools he is given and is he capable of using them in a stressful situation? The media can also affect his development. Since the average age in pro soccer has gone down, it makes sense to have this conversation sooner."

> Which psychological tools should a youth performance soccer coach be given to ensure the optimal training of young talent?

"No one can guarantee optimal training because the young players are subject to many other factors: In what environment does the talent grow up? How does he behave at school? What group does he spend his very limited free time with? A coach cannot influence these factors. People should be critical of the fact that coaches are assigned tasks such as the entire personal development. Of 100% total time, a coach only spends 20-30% with players on a daily basis. The rest of the time they are at school, at home, or in another environment. Aiming for optimal training only works in cooperation

with teachers, parents, the talent, a possible agent, and the coach. There should be reasonable communication between these parties. And to signal to the other areas: You also have a certain amount of responsibility, and soccer can't take care of everything. This requires the empowerment of the coach within the club, because it is often difficult to broach certain subjects and convey them. To do so, the coach needs the necessary self-confidence to be able to get his point across in a reasonable manner and back it up with facts. Every support benefits the talent."

> **Advisors are becoming more and more important in youth soccer.**

"The coaches must also include them in the designated communication model.

The advisors have the job and obligation to systematically develop a talent long term while not focusing on the question, how can I make as much money as possible off a player? That is a completely wrong approach. This means having empathy for the player, being able to see things from the player's perspective—what it all means to the player—and at the same time recognizing the club's wants and needs. Then the player, the club, and player's advisor benefit long term."

"COACHES MUST LEARN TO DEAL WITH DIFFICULT PLAYERS"

> **Are there more opportunities for improvement in diverse areas at the youth performance centers?**

"It must be noted that the youth development has been driven by the DFB since 2000 and that it has stayed the course in spite of lots of opposition, and this is important for German soccer.

When looking at the youth performance centers in Germany one thing is obvious: All of them have ethical guidelines, and the children and adolescents are largely clever enough to know how they must behave to stay in the system. The question remains: Can we bring in all of the young talent, or do we reject those that don't fit into the compressed concept but can make the difference in a game?

Having to learn to deal with difficult players is the problem of the present age and a major challenge for coaches. A coach must use each player's individuality and integrate it profitably into the team structure. This means that coaches have to deal much more closely with the individual characters. A coach must be able to see and treat each player as a separate individual. One might require the proverbial kick in the pants, while another might require more care. For clubs and coaches this is the challenge of the future, because these player types are able to significantly raise a team's quality. And every club wants that."

Ideally, children and adolescents of different age groups should approach the different functions in soccer with joy and enthusiasm. Of course, there are situations that can cause doubt, anxiety, or fear. We have addressed this topic and have selected a few of the many conversations with different age groups for Werner Mickler to respond to:

> Manuel, age 13: How does one stay calm while having to take the decisive penalty kick?

Try to work out a program that shows what the individual steps must look like and implement it at practice. Take the ball and position it at the penalty spot. How many steps do you take for your run-up? Where do you want the ball to go? How do you celebrate after the goal? Once you achieve that certainty at practice you will automatically be calmer when you step up and still remain focused, increasing the odds of scoring.

> David, age 14: How do you regain your confidence after you already played several bad passes in a game and are afraid to call for the ball?

Mistakes happen—that is a normal part of soccer and happens to every player in the Bundesliga and the Champions League. What's important is that you learn to handle mistakes and still have the courage to get open, to signal you are open, and to call for the ball. When you get the ball, play a clean return pass or pass it to another player. By doing so, you will regain confidence. Use every training unit to improve your passing game and boost your confidence and courage so you can then employ them advantageously in a game.

> Jonas, age 10: My coach constantly scolds me and makes me very anxious. I don't know what to do.

You should talk to the coach and, if necessary, ask a third person to be there. That will provide feedback so you can find out if the coach is even aware of it, or if you just perceive it that way. It is important to address the issue. Does the coach bite everybody's head off, or is it just your head? Maybe he also praises you, but you feel like he only criticizes you. It is important to find out and reach a mutual solution.

> Luca, age 15: Next Sunday is the cup final. I am very anxious and nervous before the game. How do I achieve a top performance?

Try to imagine situations in which you have been successful and where you were able to manage your nervousness. A certain amount of nervousness and tension is actually not a bad thing but is normal and even a positive for achieving an optimal performance. But it should not lead to sleeplessness or your anxiety having a negative effect on your ability to concentrate. It's an important game, and you should look forward to it.

> Paul, age 16: I often have to be the captain of my team. I actually don't want to be the loudest one but would rather hang back. How can a quiet player find the courage to get loud?

You should have a conversation with your coach, and he will tell you why he chose you to be captain. The coach may see certain things in you that make you the right person for the job. He may see abilities in you that you are not yet aware of. And you don't have to be loud to perform your duties as captain. Talking to the coach will give you some insight.

You don't have to completely change, but rather realize your abilities. That can be an absolute strength, and your teammates may also see it that way. But it would be different if it inhibits and freezes you while you play. If you see this duty as a mental overload, you must let your coach know.

81

> Luisa, age 12: I am now in high school and have more homework than I used to. Time-wise I am barely able to manage practice and school. But I don't want to give up soccer. How can I reconcile the two?

It is about optimizing your time management. It requires communication between the two areas and, ideally, the teacher, coach, and you sit down and figure out solutions. Make a plan beforehand as to what would work best for you, but of course school is the top priority. When you plan your time sensibly, there most likely is a way, but that may require you giving up other recreational activities (e.g., friends).

> Thomas, age 11: My coach is also my father. I feel like he is much stricter with me than the others. He constantly scolds me.

It's not an easy situation for your father, either. Of course your dad doesn't want any favoritism within the group, which is why he may treat you more harshly to avoid making himself vulnerable to the others. Talk to him so he can better understand how you feel, even if he may not like it.

If it doesn't change after you talk to him, it might make sense to switch to a different coach and a different team.

> Mauricio, age 15: Bastian Schweinsteiger is my role model. How do I acquire a winner mentality like his?

If Bastian is your role model, what does that mean? What else, aside from his winner mentality? He was frequently injured and had to work hard to get back in shape, which means he learned to meet obstacles head on and fought his way back. He has won lots of important titles. But don't forget that he has also suffered bitter and painful losses like, for instance, at the Champions League final in 2012 when he missed his penalty kick and lost. What matters is that he grew and emerged stronger. Particularly significant is the World Cup final where he was subjected to hard fouls but always got back up and never gave up. Conversely, for you this means that you must take every training unit seriously in order to get better and that you cannot let setbacks discourage you. Then you have taken an important step toward a winner mentality.

Bastian Schweinsteiger with a cut below his right eye during the 2014 World Cup final

> Philipp, age 16: In the past three months, I was ejected twice. I am actually rather quiet, but in a game I frequently can't keep my aggression under control. What should I do?

A healthy amount of aggression is generally a positive when it is used prudently in the right situations. Think about where you can use that aggression. Using it against the opponent or the ref is disadvantageous. Your team needs you, and by getting ejected, you do damage to yourself and your team. Use your energy in a positive way, like shaking off the opponent in a game or toward the end of the game when you are tired, overcoming that fatigue and taking on a "now-more-than-ever" attitude. Then you are using aggressiveness in a positive way. When you notice the aggression resurfacing in a negative way, put up a mental stop sign that says "this far and no farther."

> Mert, age 15: My coach told me that I won't move up to the U17. I am devastated and am considering quitting soccer

Ask yourself this question: Why did you begin to play soccer? You have now had a bad experience, and it is normal that you need to process it. But what matters is the fun and joy you get from this sport. Yet you should not question your goals. If you change clubs, look at it as an interim phase. Maybe you can learn more and benefit from a different coach. But you can still take bigger steps at 16 or 18, and I hope you make the right choice.

3.8 BVB-PRACTICED CONSISTENCY

Mario Götze played on nearly all the youth teams and at age 17 managed the jump to the pros.

Marcel Schmelzer, Nuri Sahin, Erik Durm, and Marian Sarr; Dortmund-born players Kevin Großkreutz and Marco Reus (left to right)

Borussia Dortmund is one of the most successful German teams in men's soccer. Next to national championship titles and successes at the DFB cup, BVB won the Champions League in 1997. The then 17-year-old Lars Ricken emerged from the youth team and in the final against Juventus Torino scored in a 3-1 preliminary decision. Borussia Dortmund remained his only club in men's soccer. Today he is the youth coordinator at BVB and oversees the talent who want to make it to the top.

Today Lars Ricken is the youth coordinator at BVB.

Lars Ricken: "Dortmund is a good example of permeability. Because when four to five players from our own youth stand on the field it creates a special affinity between team and fans. Of course, we want to drive development forward as quickly as possible, but it is also important that the boys get as much time as necessary so they don't burn out at a young age. With their workload and daily schedule, players must be mentally tough when they reach men's soccer."

The coach is closely linked to the philosophy that is practiced within the club. Jürgen Klopp, who was head coach for the 1st Bundesliga team from 2008 to 2015 and had a significant part in the cross-team conception all the way to the lower youth teams and facilitated permeability in the pro teams, says:

"The essential criteria are hunger and talent. That's not an exclusion criterion when the players are all young."

Jürgen Klopp explained his team's playing concept, which is also being implemented in the developing teams, as follows:

The BVB coach "propagates a soccer experience with lots of emotion, passion, and volition based on a strong willingness to run and tactical discipline." He talks about "recognition value" and the odd "full-throttle event." He is quoted as demanding "extreme ball-oriented defense, fast transitions in both directions, extreme versatility during possession, and fast, target-oriented forward play."[50]

Michael Zorc also came from the BVB youth program and actively played from 1981 to 1988. Today he is manager at BVB: "The most fun is when we are able to move a young player from our own youth through from the bottom up so he can start for Borussia Dortmund in front of 80,000 spectators. That's a great feeling!"

Hannes Wolf

German U17 National Champion

---

50   *Kicker*, May 2008, p. 44.

3.8.1   Insights into BVB's approach by U19 coach, Hannes Wolf

Black/yellow guideline for training: The principle of holism, where all building blocks within the training elements are practiced, applies here. In doing so, particular emphasis is placed on enthusiasm and joy of playing, providing the daily impetus for optimal improvement.

Content of the soccer-training concept: In line with the professional division. Keywords are: counter-pressing, collective, ball-oriented defense, looking deep first, quick transition to offense at top speed, aggressiveness, compactness, speed, and enthusiasm.

Here the focus is on the type of soccer, and, therefore, no system is specified. That allows us some variability and flexibility. It also includes polyvalent training of the players and no rigid positional requirements. Some positions, such as central defender, are excluded.

Implementation in daily training: Certain core exercises related to key content are taken on by the pros. Alternating and varying tasks during practice place higher demands on players in terms of attentiveness and concentration.

Sensitive phase in U17: During puberty, performance fluctuations and constitutional changes take place that must be monitored full-time, and of course the goal is for the players to come out of this phase of life stronger.

Talent prediction for pro soccer: We make these with caution because there are no guarantees. No one is written off, but decisions are made during the respective phase. Decisions are made as a group, meaning the head of youth soccer, the scout, and the coaches from the respective age groups.

There are cases when players change clubs because their current performance isn't up to par. Due to the density of professionally managed training clubs in the area, players may move into different hands, but even if they are released from Borussia Dortmund, they are still picked up. And in case of improvement, the path back to BVB is always an option.

The respective top talent is, of course, identified, and his subsequent path is regularly adjusted within the areas of responsibility. Here the path usually looks different. It is possible that a top talent plays on a U19 team while also completing training units with the pros to see top-level performances. The excellent infrastructure (everything on one campus) promotes the principle of short distances and leads to a close exchange of views and cooperation.

Example: National U17 team player. Due to the additional workload of international games and DFB training courses, he will initially remain in U17 to avoid overloading. This requires targeted monitoring of the training load, especially on the part of the club, that is provided by the professional environment.

Permeability: Demands on the young talent have gone up significantly in recent years. We, therefore, strengthen the players and try to provide them with the tools that will help them prevail. The idea that players who come from our own youth program will be supported accordingly is firmly established in our club's philosophy. But in the end it is always the individual quality of the players that counts.

Relationship between recovery and effort: This is a very important topic in daily life with the young talent. Due to the modified school system (shortened school days), the demands on the players who are also students are immense. That is why we do a daily team practice in the evening. But our players from the boarding school or youth center have additional individual training plans for the weight room or the Footbonaut. One of my jobs as coach is to manage the workload purposefully and individually and to teach the players strategies for stress management to prevent permanent overloading.

Footbonaut

A Footbonaut is a training machine that is used primarily for individual training. The player stands on a square of artificial turf while balls are played to him from all different positions and directions. He must convert the balls and after reacting to visual signals, must pass them accurately. Action speed, hardness, and ball spin can be controlled individually. The coach adjusts the exact parameters. This makes it possible to quickly and easily achieve a much higher training intensity than on a normal field under normal conditions.

Competitive situation in the West: Scouting is very intensive and is actively monitored by us coaches. Due to the club density (Schalke, Gladbach, Leverkusen, Cologne), recruiting of talent is extremely competitive.

This is a positive for players. No one has to drive more than 62 miles, and all of the clubs benefit from the extremely high quality during the national championship. As a result, the players have to give it their all in every contest and are consequently challenged and sponsored at a high level.

Title as a seal of quality: The fight for first place motivates young people, and we want to win every game as well as project a winner mentality. But most important here is what our game should look like, and we can never lose sight of that in training.

We use technical support like video analysis to improve as a team and individually. But it also helps us to specifically prepare for each opponent. It is a way for us to provide our players with the tools for each game and, in doing so, achieve a degree of variability and flexibility that improves the players individually and as a team.

3.8.2   Youth soccer coach as a full-time job

EXAMPLE OF U19 COACH HANNES WOLF'S WEEKLY SCHEDULE	
Monday:	
9 am	Meeting with colleagues for opponent analysis
11 am	Informal gathering at the office with youth leadership and scouting department (review previous weekend)
Noon-4 pm	Video analysis of own game and weekly planning
4-5 pm	Meeting with physical therapist and athletic coach (state of health and training planning)
5-6 pm	Specific training preparation with assistant coach and goalkeeping coach/greet players
6-7:40 pm	Team practice
7:40-8 pm	Contemplate the practice

EXAMPLE OF U19 COACH HANNES WOLF'S WEEKLY SCHEDULE	
Tuesday:	
	Attempt to take the day off
Wednesday:	
9 am	Arrive at the office
9 am-1 pm	Video analysis of opponent and entry of weekend game into database
3-4 pm	Work out strategy for next game
4-5 pm	Meeting with physical therapist and athletic coach (state of health and training planning)
5-6 pm	Specific training preparation with assistant coach and goalkeeping coach/greet players
6-7:40 pm	Team practice
7:40-8 pm	Contemplate the practice
Thursday:	
9 am-1 pm	Structural/content work at the office
4-5 pm	Meeting with physical therapist and athletic coach (state of health and training planning)
5-6 pm	Specific training preparation with assistant coach and goalkeeping coach/greet players
6-7:40 pm	Team practice
7:40-8 pm	Contemplate the practice
Friday:	
4-5 pm	Meeting with physical therapist and athletic coach (state of health and training planning)
5-6 pm	Specific training preparation with assistant coach and goalkeeping coach/greet players
6-7:40 pm	Team practice
7:40-8 pm	Contemplate the practice

EXAMPLE OF U19 COACH HANNES WOLF'S WEEKLY SCHEDULE	
Saturday:	
10 am	Arrive at training ground
10-11 am	Planning of final practice
11 am-12:20 pm	Practice
12:45-1:30 pm	Group lunch/video analysis/announcement of squad and lineup
Sunday:	
	Home games: meet 1.5 hours before game; away games: meeting place subject to opponent and joint travel to venue
11 am	Championship game

Different, irregular activities are integrated into this weekly cycle:

- National and international scouting

- Meetings with players, families, and advisors of interested players (sometimes for several days)

- Monitoring training and play of U16 and U17 national teams (national and international)

- Observation of professional training to bring in line/improve training and playing philosophy

- Exchange of content and information with colleagues at Borussia Dortmund (fellow coaches, teachers, psychologists, scouts, youth leadership)

3.9 DILIGENCE, INTERNATIONAL FLAIR, AND BLOOD, SWEAT, AND TEARS-SCHALKE 04'S YOUTH DIVISION BUILDS PROS

3.9.1 Interview with Schalke's director of youth development, Oliver Ruhnert

> The *Knappenschmiede* (miner's forge) is one of the most successful training centers in Germany. What is so special about Schalke 04's talent development?

Oliver Ruhnert

"Just like the other youth performance centers, we try to employ highly qualified coaches who can push our talent forward in the technical–tactical area and also in their personal development. Our advantage is the affinity for our club, Schalke 04. We work with the players every day in close proximity to the stadium and give them the sense that Schalke is something special. That is also the reason for the special name of our department, which stands for our lived tradition."

> Talent is a prerequisite for making it into a youth performance center. Are there any other scouting criteria that are essential to being accepted by you?

"I would not say essential. We also make compromises when we decide to sign players. When we recruit a player with an exceptional left foot, we will take him in spite of some other deficiencies. Moreover, we also evaluate the player's temperament during observation. How does the player react to a lead or a point deficit? How does the player behave during warm-up? What is his social behavior within the group? The answers to these questions enter into our overall evaluation."

Homegrown in the Knappenschmiede: Benedikt Höwedes, Joel Matip, Julian Draxler, Max Meyer, and Leroy Sané

> Kevin-Prince Boateng and Sead Kolasinac, who is from the own youth, are two pro players who were not always "low-maintenance" in their youth, but are characters. Should we make more allowances for individual characters in training rather than practice leveling-down?

"Of course there are always discussions about whether or not we need more characters in German soccer. One focus of our training is to look at each player as an individual. It is important to not just penalize a young player, but to influence him pedagogically and socially and, thus, give him a chance. With respect to Sead, I can honestly say that we are glad to have brought him to Schalke 04 and that our investment in him has paid off."

> With Christian Rubio Sivodedov you have signed a major 17-year-old Swedish talent who was also wooed by other clubs. What made the difference for Schalke?

"We are absolutely convinced of Christian's potential and worked very hard to sign him. Of course, we knew that other prestigious clubs also courted Christian. The process was likely no different from other clubs. He stayed at the hotel, looked at everything, and met the people in charge. But when we were at the stadium together and watched a game, he met the people, and he realized that this club is something special. Schalke 04 showed him a clear path that we will walk down together. We told him that he won't be with the pros right away but should play with the U19 first to get acclimated. We have to take into consideration that he has only just turned 17. He is learning a new language, is getting used to his environment, and we will take the necessary time and patience to develop him. He was impressed with our explicit plan, and that is why he chose us."

> Courting talent is starting increasingly earlier. U13 players are switching within Germany and also to other countries. As a club, what is your position on the subject?

"We don't do that here, and I find this development alarming. We are in a region of approximately 6 million people, and if we were unable to win young players for our club from that portfolio, we would be doing something wrong. Throughout Germany and certainly throughout Europe, it is our duty to keep an eye out for top talent, but not for 13-year-olds. We have a definite opinion on the subject and don't accept any players younger than 15 into our boarding school."

"WE ARE CONVINCED OF THE EXCELLENCE OF OUR COACHES"

> Do the individual training levels have a consistent playing philosophy?

"No! That's where we are different from other clubs. Due to changes in the head coach position in the professional area in recent years, we have approached that differently. Of course, our performance teams must practice and master the systematics and playing philosophy of the pros so the players are able to adapt more quickly at the top. That's a given. Otherwise, we do things our own way. The coaches have the flexibility to use different systems and the liberty to move within them. We are convinced of the excellence of our coaches and their ability to find the right approach."

> Is there anything particular about choosing coaches for youth teams?

"The basic prerequisite is the appropriate license and, thus, an important precept for a coach to even be of interest to Schalke 04. We want a mix of emotional coaches and developmental coaches who can work conceptually, who are able teach different formations and provide the players with different courses of action. It is very important for the coach to be able to react to different situations in a game. I want a youth coach who can get actively involved in a game and not just sit on the bench for 90 minutes and then analyze the match afterward. Being active means providing support to the

youth players, not permanently, but situationally. It is important that I have a coach who embodies that. I am also selective, which is why we have had some turnovers, because we are looking for the best. We have an U19 coach who has done very successful work for many years. We aspire to being the best in all areas, and for that reason we also want to continue to improve our coaches."

> As a traditional club, Schalke has enormous appeal to its many fans and also a high media presence. Is it possible to specifically prepare the top talent who are about to join the pros?

"No, not completely! With the introduction of the U19 youth league, the boys have experienced increased media attention, which they had to and could handle. We played in front of more spectators than in the A Youth Bundesliga. We also try to provide them with courses of action through individual conversations and also through media training. But it is difficult to simulate the situation of running onto the field in a sold-out stadium, and that's why we do everything to prepare them in the best possible way. But what they do with that in the end depends on their character."

> At the U19, youth cup teams compete on an international level. Can these games be compared to the A Youth Bundesliga?

"There are teams in the youth league that are better, but there are also teams like Maribor, who would probably play for relegation in the Bundesliga. We had a narrow loss in a penalty shootout against Manchester City, and the level of play in that game was dauntingly high. That definitely helps the boys improve, and that is why that competition is important and useful to us. It is difficult to compare the two competitions."

> What is the feedback from clubs like Barcelona or Chelsea regarding training in Germany?

"On the one hand, there is a Europe-wide evaluation of this competition and, of course, also communication between the responsible parties from the various clubs. It has been noticed that we are getting a lot of respect for the way we play soccer because we do it differently. When you look at most of the players who take the field on these teams, they are international select teams that have been assembled with lots of money. You can't even compare that to our financial means. When we talk about clubs like Barcelona, Manchester

City, or Chelsea, we are worlds apart. From a sports perspective, it is interesting that we are largely able to not only keep up in these games, but have also won, which speaks for our training. The training in Germany is highly regarded in other countries.

"THE TRAINING IN GERMANY IS HIGHLY REGARDED IN OTHER COUNTRIES"

Arsenal London, in particular, asked to sit in with us to pick up some of our expertise and to answer the question of why German soccer training is so successful. The fact that the English are looking to the German model shows that English soccer has some catching up to do."

> The Premier International Cup is largely unknown in Germany. Next to Schalke 04, Gladbach is the only other Bundesliga team participating. What were the reasons for participating?

"We accepted an invitation by the Premier League. We saw it as an opportunity for our players to continue to compete on the international level after the A Youth. But the problem we had that year was the injury problems of the pros. Horst Heldt's and my original idea was to also use the games for our top talent who don't get a lot of playing time. Due to the staff shortage, that was, unfortunately, not possible."

> What can we learn from other countries to keep a top spot in training?

"The top international clubs provide a level of infrastructure for their training teams that we just can't touch. Sports medicine is also at a much higher level. Besides, they have a lot more specialty coaches than we do. We have determined this based on our observations. Whether or not that's the right answer is being discussed. It is a fact that they put incredible effort into their training. When you visit Sporting Lisbon or Manchester, you can feel the enormous value these clubs place on training."

> Based on the DFL decision, the U23 teams will only exist on a volunteer basis in the Bundesliga. You stand by that decision. Why?

"We wanted a team between the pros and U19. We are not real happy with the current constellation of the five regional leagues. Admittedly, the Regional League West is still one of the strongest, but we still haven't come to any conclusion. The players also come

from the U19 with their international experiences and are used to other conditions. They have trouble adapting to the level of play and the opponents in the league. We are having an internal debate on how to handle this matter in the future. But we definitely want to preserve the U23."

> The transition is a big step for the talent. Players who change teams and after training units or appearances with the pros are back to playing U19 or play in the U23. How does the club communicate these matters, and do you have someone who only looks after the top talent?

"Of course we have someone who takes care of the top talent exclusively. The communication you mentioned is a key concept that we live by every day at the club. We have very close communication with the individual levels, especially with the sports director, Horst Heldt.

"DILIGENCE IS REWARDED DOWN THE ROAD"

The coaches of the U19 and U23 performance teams and the pros communicate daily about our top talent and all steps are discussed as a group. We meet with the entire team at least once a month, including the pro's head coach, and talk about different issues. And, of course, there are always desires, and it is not possible to always satisfy all sides.

We consider it a success that in recent years so many young players have integrated into the professional team. Prerequisite was and is the absolute desire of the staff to develop our own talent within the cub and guide them to the top. And that is the main requirement for becoming a coach at Schalke 04. While the name might have changed, this criterion is one of the essential points for a head coach at Schalke."

> Does the club have an idea of how many players from its own youth are on the professional squad?

"We don't have a quota we must meet, but currently there are 13 players from the Knappenschmiede. We rank our top talent within the respective age groups and look at who in the respective positions might be of interest to the pros in the years ahead. Our transfer policy is, to some extent, also geared to that. If, as an example, from our perspective we develop a top talent as a right-back and the prognosis for the future looks

good, we will not sign a player who, as a back-up, might arrest our player's development. In individual cases, loans are also an option if analysis shows that a player isn't yet ready for the first team but is not sufficiently challenged in the regional league. Precondition is that the player will have regular appearances at the club that wants him. That makes sense for everyone involved."

> **The professional sector is booming, but volunteers have been decreasing for years. How does that affect a professional club?**

"It definitely affects us. Schalke 04 is still a registered association, meaning that we are obligated to meet our not-for-profit obligations as established in our bylaws. But it is not just for that reason that it is important for us to have many volunteer staff at our club. But they are usually older. For younger people, it isn't necessarily a given any more. We will also need to address that issue in the future."

> **Any predictions regarding the top talent?**

"Even with all of our top experts, it is still difficult to predict whether a top talent will make it. Some players who were poised to make the leap did not make it for various reasons, while other less likely players suddenly take off. But if there's one word for the players who do make it, it would have to be diligence. Players who work hard on themselves, who go out before practice or stay after practice, are more likely to succeed. Diligence is rewarded down the road. We have also talked about players where we asked ourselves: Why is he not making it? We believe that certain players don't give their all to really make it to the top. They like to come to practice,

It gets narrower at the top.

participate cheerfully, do their job pretty well, but don't put their heart and soul into it. To us that is a critical factor."

3.10 AT THE THRESHOLD TO PRO SOCCER – LIFE AFTER THE YOUTH PERFORMANCE CENTER

Everyone is talking about the youth performance centers in Germany. It is where the Bundesliga of tomorrow is being trained with a speed and dependability that, with few exceptions, is unparalleled in Europe and the world. But who actually makes it from the A Youth to the pros? What are the critical factors? Schalke's captain Benedikt Höwedes recently publicly criticized the German youth performance centers' reliable products: "Young players today sometimes lack a certain humility that we had in our day. They are demanding but don't have the extreme ambition we needed to even gain a foothold in the pros. Back then, not as many young players moved up; we had to work harder to do so. Today I see relatively many young players who just rely on their talent and then lack that final punch."[51]

Bayern Munich superstar Arjen Robben takes the same line: "Nowadays there are boys who play their first game at age 19 or 20 and think they've made it. That's wrong! There is always room for improvement, no matter how old you are."[52] The way to the top is difficult and full of setbacks. Only those who have learned to deal with defeats and emerge stronger might one day have a chance to make it to the pros.

Arjen Robben

And that depends on different factors. Next to patience, it certainly requires hard work and tenacity. Schalke captain Benedikt Höwedes warns of bringing young players up too soon: "It is generally good for players to enjoy sustainable basic training before joining the pros. That is how it was with our generation. Today some of them train at the top very early on. And when it becomes apparent that they just don't have it yet, they have to move back down. For some that's hard to process."[53] Robben agrees with the Schalke world champion: "You have to be mentally strong. But it is

51   Interview with Benedikt Höwedes: "Many young players rest on their laurels." 2014, *kicker sports magazine*, p. 13.
52   Quote from *Bild Online*, 2015. Available at: www.bild.de/sport/fussball/bayern-muenchen/arjen-robben-kritisiert-junge-spieler-39778086.
53   Interview with Benedikt Höwedes: "Many young players rest on their laurels." 2014, *kicker sports magazine*, p. 13.

also very important to be self-critical. That's something I don't see much of in the younger generation."[54]

The critical requirement to ultimately come out on top is constant ambition to get better. At least that's how superstar Arjen Robben sees it, Robben trains with such dedication, obsessiveness, and meticulousness as is rarely seen among players to date: "I learn from him [Pep Guardiola] every day, and that's special. Even at ages 26 and 27, you can still make major progress."[55]

Lots of talent flounder during the transition to senior soccer. There are a number of players each year who come from youth soccer, but there are few spots in the highest leagues. Those are at a premium and fiercely contested. The list of those who don't make it to the pros is far longer than the names you later see in the newspaper. But signing a pro soccer contract does not mean that you have pro status. Jos Luhukay, former coach at Hertha BSC, says it like this: "Getting on a pro team is only the first step. Getting established there is much more difficult."[56]

The players confront many changes and influences that must first be lived through. That starts with the first practice with the pros. The differences in terms of tempo, playing speed, rigor, and physicality are huge, and the adjustment process can take a while. But the young players face many more challenges. Everything rains down on the young players: media, environment, expectations, pressure, cars, money, advisors, and external competition as well as competition inside their own team.

Reinhold Yabo has lived through these phases. He was captain of the German U20 junior national team and was unable to establish himself right away at 1. FC Cologne. He, therefore, took the detour to the 2nd Bundesliga at Karlsruhe SC and there advanced to an absolute key player. He talks about his experiences:

Reinhold Yabo, Captain of the German U20 side

---

54   Quote from *Bild Online*, 2015.
55   Quote from "Arjen Robben kritisiert junge Spieler: They think they've made it after just one game" *Bild Online*, 2015.
56   *Tagesspiegel Online*. Available at: http://www.tagesspiegel.de/themen/hertha-bsc/hertha-bsc-und-der-nachwuchs-hertha-trainer-luhukay-verfolgt-das-prinzip-fordern-und-foerdern/9520570-2.html.

"Many become star players from one day to the next, get new contracts, or suddenly make lots of money. You think you're on top of the world. Coming into pro soccer can fundamentally change the character of young players. I did not realize that the difference between juniors and the pros is so huge. Many factors come to bear here: the necessary ounce of luck, the right coach, top performance at the right time, sometimes the injury of an experienced player in the same position, and you are there at the right moment."[57]

That is why young players should ask themselves every day:

How do I deal with my profession? What does my self-assessment look like? Am I too easily satisfied with what I have achieved? The first success: When will I be a pro? With my first appearance? After 10 appearances? Later than that?

> *"Always keep your love for soccer alive, develop confidence in your intuition, only think about the next step, don't set your sights too high, turn weaknesses into strengths, enjoy being a part of a team, recognize your own potential, find the right support."*
>
> —Philipp Lahm[58]

The reasons why young players fail are very diverse. Some lack the necessary appreciation and humility, others the patience and desire, the necessary discipline, and still others are not self-critical enough, possess little self-control, and lack team spirit. Norbert Elgert, who, as Schalke U19 coach, is already a club legend and has made players like Manuel Neuer, Benedikt Höwedes, Mesut Özil, Julian Draxler, and Max Meyer into pros with his precision touch, has a similar view: "There is no secret to success. We are all subject to humility. You need to look at the big picture. It's a constant struggle against pressure of space, opponent, and time. And most importantly: The head wins. If, as a young player, you don't have the necessary mental toughness, you will not be able to realize your dream. A Bundesliga game means enormous pressure."[59]

---

57   *11 Freunde* online interview, 2015. Available at: http://www.11freunde.de/interview/einmal-super-talent-und-zurueck-reinhold-yabo-vom-ksc.

58   A fine difference, p. 25

59   Quote from *WAZ*, 2013. Available at: http://www.derwesten.de/sport/fussball/s04/wir-muessen-demuetig-bleiben-id7603310.html.

In that regard, Dr. Jens Rehhagel, director of the Hannover 96 youth performance center, makes the case primarily for patience: "The age structure of the players who play in the Bundesliga has shifted upward. As a result, there is often a sense of impatience. But that doesn't come from the club. Most of the time we are the ones who try to eliminate the pressure and the pace. Our coaches see the players every day and make assessments as to who needs to work on what, and it is critical that the coaches work through these individual developmental steps together with the players based on these assessments. It is important to achieve continuous development so the players are constantly improving. For many young players, impatience has rarely resulted in success because skipping over certain fundamentals could not compensated for."

The paths taken here by the various professional soccer clubs within the transition phase differ greatly.

At the league association's members meeting in March 2014, two-thirds of the Bundesliga clubs voted for their own decision-making authority with respect to the deregistration of U23 teams and, thus, decided to "expand their courses of action regarding youth teams" in the future.[60] The reason given was "the considerably improved level of training in youth performance centers." Simply, this means that many U23 teams are not sufficiently challenged in the 4th League. During the 2014/2015 season, three Bundesliga clubs— Mainz, Dortmund, and Stuttgart—had a second representation in the 3rd League. Thus, in the future, it will be up to each club to either retain an U23 team or eliminate it.

Eintracht Frankfurt and Bayer Leverkusen were the first Bundesliga clubs to deregister their U23. Rudi Völler, executive sports director at Bayer Leverkusen, says about the reasons why: "We had to recognize that our top talent would not be able to make the jump to a Bundesliga team via a second team in the 4th League."[61]

Instead, Bayer 04 Leverkusen has chosen the path of having their hopefuls on loan: current cases are Christoph Kramer (Mönchengladbach) and Dominik Kohr (Augsburg). This model was already successfully applied in the past with Stefan Reinartz (then at Nürnberg).

---

60   Available at: http://www.fupa.net/berichte/bayer-04-darf-seine-u23-abschaffen-135986.html.
61   *Bayer 04 Leverkusen online*. Available at: http://www.bayer04.de/804-DEU/de/_md_aktuell-dt. aspx?aktuell=aktuell-10171.

By contrast, other clubs made positive experiences with the U23. Patrick Herrmann, Jonathan Schmid, Maximilian Philipp, Robin Knoche, or the Khedira brothers are just a few examples of players who started their Bundesliga career on an U23 team.

Dr. Jens Rehhagel, director of the Hannover 96 youth performance center, considers the U23 a vital part of talent development: "We absolutely need our U23 and have a definite position on this issue. Very few manage to move directly from A Youth to the pros. For those players, it is important to get a lot of playing practice in the regional league and be able to assert themselves at a decent level. They need this developmental step to acclimate themselves to other men's teams. Moreover, we have current examples of pros that are integrated into our U23 after injuries or if they have little practical experience. It is, therefore, indispensable to our club's philosophy."

But there are also plenty of examples of other paths: Mario Götze, Julian Draxler, Timo Werner, Matthias Ginter, or Maximilian Arnold are examples of those players who made the direct leap to the pros from the U19. Robin Knoche, on the other hand, took the U23 detour to the pros. This shows that the paths that can be successful can be very different— as happens so often in soccer.

Mario Götze *Julian Draxler* *Timo Werner* *Robin Knoche* *Maximilian Arnold*

Hoffenheim's director of pro soccer, Alexander Rosen, also defends the existence of the U23: "For us, the U23 is an ideal development team where our best talent from the academy and the young players from the pro squad get important competitive playing time at a good level." Former Dortmund coach, Jürgen Klopp, criticizes the elimination of the U23: "It's a catastrophe. I don't think it's ok that the league association's general assembly allowed this to happen. Different clubs are now giving the 19-year-olds the message, if you haven't made it yet, you never will."[62]

62 Quote from *kicker online*. Available at: http://www.t-online.de/sport/fussball/id_70503172/abschaffung-der-u23-teams-fuer-juergen-klopp-eine-katastrophe-.html.

Borussia Mönchengladbach also prefers a consistently open path of which the U23 is a significant component: "We continue to follow the openness principle from youth to pros. Since our move to the Borussia Park in July 2001, an average of 20 young players from our own youth have made it into the Bundesliga. That's an average of two per year."[63]

Michael Reschke, technical director at FC Bayern Munich and previously a squad planner at Bayer Leverkusen for 35 years, is an expert in this area and does not see a "silver bullet" to the top for the young players. "There are many paths that can lead to success. For Christoph Kramer, it was being on loan; for Marco Reus, the development through Dortmund, Ahlen, Gladbach, and then back to Dortmund. For Phillipp Lahm, it was the detour through Stuttgart. On the other hand, Manuel Neuer already had a regular berth at Schalke 04 at a young age. Salzburg was probably ideal for Kevin Kampl. He needed a longer maturing process." And on the subject of on-loan players: "Bayern Munich does not loan players as a matter of principle, but rather on a case-by-case basis. We weigh very carefully what makes the most sense for a young player".[64]

This diversity, in particular, seems to be a decisive factor in whether or not a player is able to make the leap into the professional leagues. The clubs that are able to make the best case-by-case decisions will benefit most from the development of the players. Indisputable is—and all sides stress this—that next to the luck of choosing the right path, a lot of hard daily training is required.

---

63 *kicker.* Available at: http://www.kicker.de/news/fussball/bundesliga/startseite/618528/artikel_eberl-erntet-die-fruechte-seiner-%28jugend-%29arbeit.html.

64 *Zeit Online.* Available at: http://www.zeit.de/news/2015-01/13/fussball-reschke-fc-bayern-darf-kein-talente-verleih-werden-13085605.

PART 3: EXAMPLES

4
MANY ROADS LEAD TO THE TOP

We will use five examples to show that there is not that one path to the Bundesliga. Particularly in performance soccer, many athletes are frequently subject to major setbacks—not being considered on game days, a dip in form, injuries, or upheaval in the player's environment. A talent's path to the pros is long and hard. Some crack in the process; others overcome all obstacles with ease only to falter at the final hurdle before the goal. And yet others make their way to performance soccer with work, tenacity, and a particular kind of resilience.

> *"It is hard. An athlete's will is important. Many players have the physical requirements, the technique, the speed. But the psyche, the character... that's crucial!"*
>
> —Christian Streich[65]

---

65   Interview with Christian Streich in *DIE ZEIT*, Oct. 21, 2013.

4.1 MANUEL NEUER– THE BOY FROM BUER STARTS THE GOALKEEPER REVOLUTION

Manuel Neuer was born on March 27, 1986, in Gelsenkirchen, Germany, in the Buer district. As a little boy he was able to see the Park Stadium from the attic window of his parents' house. On March 1, 1991, he became a member of Schalke 04 at the age of four and played on every youth team from Bambinis to U19. In spite of his tender age, Manuel clearly remembers those early days: "The first time I came to practice at Schalke, the coach put me in the goal. I was the smallest one and the new kid. That's how it was back then. The new kid is in the goal. It took getting used to. We practiced on black cinders. Dust clouds moved across the field in summer. The ground was rock-hard. That doesn't make goalkeeping fun. My mother had to patch my track pants multiple times. Sometimes there was blood. Scars are a part of the job. But in the beginning, I only cared about being at Schalke. When you live in Gelsenkirchen, you want to play for Schalke. You are willing to take your lumps to do so."[66] In the years ahead, Manuel continued to improve as goalkeeper, but at age 12 or 13, his career at Schalke nearly came to an end. At that time, he was still quite small and of slight build and was going to be eliminated because he did not have the desired height and build. But the goalkeeping coach and trainer at that time, Lothar Matuschak, had already noticed him and completed some talent-selection training units with him.[67] That is how he was able to convince Helmut Schulte, the youth sports director at that time, to hold on to Manuel because he felt that he showed a lot of promise with respect to soccer thinking and goalkeeping.

---

66 Quote by Waldherr in "Manuel Neuer: Our number 1," *Mobil – Deutsche Bahn Magazin*. Available at: http://mobil. deutschebahn.com/leben/unsere-nummer-1/.

67 Schmalenbach 2014: Without him, Neuer would have been eliminated. *TZ Online*, 2014. Available at: http://www.tz.de/ sport/fc-bayern/ohne-matuschak-waere-neuer-aussortiert-worden-meta-3392044.html.

"SOMETIMES THERE WAS BLOOD. SCARS ARE A PART OF THE JOB."

Along with soccer, Neuer also played club tennis until age 14. Here, too, he was considered to be highly talented. Back then, some people thought he could also have a future in tennis. But Manuel has a more humble view, although he does think that having played another sport had a positive effect on his development as goalkeeper. "The term tennis pro is an exaggeration. We didn't even have the money for advanced training. Fortunately, I chose the right sport. But tennis is good for goalkeeping. Anticipating where the ball will go, how far it will go, getting in the right position, figuring out the step sequence—like with a long cross when you stand at the short corner and have to take quick backward steps. And when you move to the net in tennis, it is similar to a 1-on-1 in soccer. These are all things that are incorporated and can be helpful. I occasionally play during the season and while on vacation, just to stay in shape and to prepare."[68]

Two goalkeeping role models influenced Neuer when he was young: "Edwin van der Sar (Manchester United) and Jens Lehmann, they were my idols. Both have a goalkeeping style that I wanted to emulate, offensive and actively engaged." As ball boy at the former Park Stadium, young Neuer stood behind Jens Lehmann's goal and watched closely: "Of course I was always closer to Jens Lehmann than van der Sar. As a Schalke fan, I felt particularly close to him. As an adolescent, I would deliberately go the stadium early to see his warm-up and exercises."[69]

Edwin van der Sar (left) and Jens Lehman (right)

Manuel trained meticulously for the aforementioned style of soccer and as a result developed a very good technique early on. In addition to his potential in the goal, he already was such a good soccer player in his youth that he was even used on the field:

---

68   Eichler, 2013, "I have a helper instinct," *FAZ Online*. Available at: http://www.faz.net/aktuell/sport/fussball/manuel-neuer-im-gespraech-ich-habe-so-einen-helferinstinkt-12107565-p3.html?printPagedArticle=true#pageIndex_3.

69   Kielbassa and Kneer, 2011, "I only have this one career," *SZ Online*. Available at: http://www.sueddeutsche.de/sport/manuel-neuer-im-gespraech-ich-habe-nur-diese-eine-karierre-1.1105577.

"That was in the B Youth against Dortmund. I had a broken finger, which is why I played on the field instead of tending goal. And I scored with a bicycle kick."[70]

The increasing number of training units in addition to school left little time for recreational activities. He gladly made sacrifices in other areas at a young age to pursue his big dream: "More than anything it has to be fun. Don't forget that I left the house at 7am, practiced after school, and did not get home until 9pm. We only had one afternoon off per week. There was little time for schoolwork. I was often afraid of getting bad grades. And during those days I lost touch with my friends. I missed parties, couldn't go on vacation. And when it was grandpa's birthday, I couldn't go to the party on Saturday."[71] After receiving his technical diploma, he devoted himself completely to his goal of becoming a pro soccer player. And soon after that he was to have his first Bundesliga appearance. The permanent goalkeeper at that time, Frank Rost, was injured. Neuer premiered on August 19, 2006, in Aachen 1-0 with a clean sheet and apparently completely composed, which he today debunks as a sham. "I was so terribly nervous", he says, "I fooled them all!"[72] After that he replaced Rost in goal and became number one.

"I FOOLED THEM ALL"

And on he went at a furious pace; 2009 marked another highlight in his career. Neuer became European champion with the U21 national team that consisted of Jerome Boateng, Benedikt Höwedes, Mats Hummels, Sami Khedira, and Mesut Özil. He was also awarded best goalkeeper in this tournament.

Two years later, after winning the DFB Cup with Schalke and 20 years of membership, Manuel switched to record champion Bayern Munich. There were tears at this official farewell press conference—understandable when you are leaving your home and your club, where you grew up. Nevertheless, from a sports perspective, it was the sensible thing to do at that time: "Back then I asked myself: How can I be the most successful? And in Munich, the preconditions for becoming successful and winning titles are better than anywhere else in the world."

After the change was announced, there were initial reservations against Manuel from the fan scene in Munich. A top club like Bayern has a different level of pressure, and he was

---

70 Eichler, 2013.
71 Waldherr, 2014.
72 Hartmann, 2008, "In the hands of a boy," *SZ*. Available at: http://www.sueddeutsche.de/sport/schalke-in-den-haenden-eines-buben-1.868236.

at the receiving end. This resulted in a difficult start, and in the beginning, he could not even get close to the stands. But his conviction and his quality soon silenced even the last critic. "Of course it has an effect. But I had been in other pressure situations, most recently during the announcement of the change and as a young captain at Schalke. It is formative. You perform, get approval, work hard, get more approval, and so on. At some point you have the self-confidence to say: 'I can do this.' By the time you have played 100 Bundesliga games and played at the international level, you have internalized that. Back then, I was resilient enough to properly handle the situation."[73] The concurrent signing of his trusted goalkeeping coach was certainly helpful: "I also have to credit Toni Tapalović for helping me become the goalkeeper I am today. He helped me develop."[74]

The success story continues. In 2013, he won the triple with Bayern Munich and in the same year was also chosen goalkeeper of the year. He internalized his new persona—the modern, actively participating goalkeeper. Pep Guardiola did not only expand and change the role of all field players at Bayern Munich, but also that of the goalkeeper. Soccer legend Zinedine Zidane had this to say: "Neuer is a fantastic player who has raised goalkeeping to another level with his offensive play. He is a phenomenon between the posts."[75]

Manuel Neuer with CL Cup

Of course, it is nice to draw praise, but it isn't Manuel's nature to set himself apart from the others: "I'm a team player. I always try to forestall, to anticipate whether one of our defenders will make an error or stand in the wrong spot. The spectators don't usually see that and wonder: Why is he coming out? I have a helper's instinct. I am prepared to iron out the mistakes of others and to take a chance. Nowadays, understanding the game is a huge factor. If you give a teammate the wrong information, he will be stand in the wrong place. You have to be able to read the game."[76]

But before he could achieve his next big goal, he experienced a setback.

73 "Neuer: Gomez in the heart, Kahn on the mind," 2011, *Sport online*. Available at: http://archiv.sport1.de/de/fussball/fussball_dfbteam/artikel_414077.html.

74 Kuhlhoff, 2013, "Soccer is never boring," *11 Freunde online*. Available at: http://www.11freunde.de/interview/manuel-neuer-ueber-den-bvb-motivtion-und-john-mcenroe.

75 Wallrodt, 2015, "Neuer is fantastic, Ronaldo like an alien," *Die Welt online*. Available at: http://www.de/sport/fussball/internationale-ligen/article137215594/Neuer-ist-fantastisch-Ronaldo-wie-ein-Alien.html.

76 Eichler, 2013.

Up to now he had been spared from injuries, but just before the World Cup in Brazil he sustained a shoulder injury. He was able to only complete individual parts of the preparation, and it was unclear whether he would be able to make it to the opening game against Portugal. "I am very impatient by nature, and I have to be able to move and get lots of exercise. For that reason it was not a good experience. But I controlled myself as best I could. And I also had some interesting experiences during that time. I was and am a positive person, and even in consultation with my doctors, I was convinced that I would be ready in time."[77] And that's what happened. Germany celebrated the World Cup title, and Manuel Neuer's saves in this tournament made him a guarantee for success. Round 16 match against Algeria was unforgettable. The suspense of that game was hard to beat. He repeatedly ensured the advance to the next round with multiple spectacular forays and sliding tackles outside the penalty box. In the aftermath, many experts called this game the key game to the title win. Neuer agrees: "One thing I know is that if I had not made those forays against Algeria, we would have been eliminated."[78]

"AS WORLD CHAMPION, NO ONE GIVES YOU AN ADVANTAGE"

But fortunately it turned out differently. Manuel also fulfilled another dream. Although he had already won (nearly) everything as goalkeeper in club soccer and celebrated the success with the national team, the fact that he ticked that off his list after the World Cup and looked ahead to the next tasks speaks volumes: "Of course I enjoy being world champion, and sometimes my mind travels back to that fantastic success. Nevertheless, now we are back to zero, and as world champion, no one gives you an advantage. Only the current season counts, and I am focused on that with all my ambition."[79] Being voted goalkeeper of the year for a second time did not seem to impress him. Perpetual learning as a pro is his goal. "I already did that back when I would watch the show Eurogoals. I was less interested in the goals that were the focus but studied the behavior of the goalkeepers. I always picked out those aspects that I thought would help me improve. And that is how I watch the games here, by always putting myself in the place of the goalkeepers. You pick out the positives and leave the negatives behind." [80]

---

77 Kübler, 2014, "Manuel Neuer: 'I see nothing of the soccer field,'" *Badische Zeitung*. Available at: http://www.badische-zeitung.de/f-wm/manuel -neuer-vom-fussballplatz-sehe-ich-nichts--85373015html.

78 Wallrodt, 2015, "My best game was a 0-0 against Freiburg," *Die Welt online*. Available at: http://www.welt.de/sport/fussball/bundesliga/fc-bayern-muenchen/article138840793/Mein-bestes-Spiel-war-ein0-0-gegen-Freiburg.html.

79 Hoeltzenbein and Selldorf, 2014, "I like to participate in play on the field," *SZ Online*. Available at: http://www.sueddeutsche.de/sport/manuel-neuer-im-interview-ich-spiele-auch-gern-im-Feld-mit-1.2123221.

80 Rosentritt, 2014, "I am not a Thomas Müller," *Der Tagesspiegel online*. Available at: http://www.tagesspiegel.de/sport/wm-2014-halbfinale-deutschland-brasilien-manuel-neuer-ich-bin-also-kein-thomas-mueller/10165396.html.

Of course, he realizes that he isn't just a public figure, but that many people see him as a role model and want to emulate him.

"I want to be a role model for children and adolescents, and also for adult fans. I think a sensible lifestyle and modesty are important. Of course, we make a lot of money, but we have to maintain a sense of reality. We cannot create the impression that only out-of-touch idiots who don't care about the world run around in soccer stadiums. I don't need a red carpet. I would rather draw attention with a good performance on the field."[81]

Manuel Neuer on his way to receive the 2014 World Cup trophy

He is aware of his beginnings and is socially active. In 2010, Neuer established the Manuel Neuer Kids Foundation that implements aid projects for disadvantaged children in the Ruhr region. One can sense that he is as invested in this project as he is in soccer:

"I gained a lot from the culture of the Ruhr region where I grew up. It is a complex society with many social fractures. When I left there, the unemployment rate was 26%. In Gelsenkirchen, 40% of the population live in poverty. I remember as a child that some kids did not go on field trips. One classmate always asked me for my lunch. Even today, many don't have warm meals. And by the way, that is true all over Germany. We pay for the school cafeteria food, offer tutoring, support music programs, hold DJ workshops, or organize summer camps. The Kids Foundation is a way for me to share my good fortune and meet my social responsibility by giving back to disadvantaged children in my homeland some of the things I was lucky enough to have in my youth: opportunities and prospects for my life.[82]

When he makes statements about his future, it becomes clear why he has, to date, achieved so much as a pro: "Once you stop improving, soccer isn't fun anymore. I try to improve every day a new."[83]

"I TRY TO IMPROVE EVERY DAY A NEW."

---

81   Waldherr, 2014.
82   *Manuel Neuer* website. Available at: http://www.manuel-neuer.com; see the yearbook of Neuer Kid Foundation. Available at: http://www.neuer-kids-foundation.de/tl_files/downloads/Jahrbuch.pdf.
83   Eichler, 2013.

4.2 NO NAME–EUROPEAN VAGABOND–WORLD CHAMPION–THE CRAZY TALE OF SHKODRAN MUSTAFI

Shkodran who? That was the likely reaction of many soccer experts on June 7, 2014, when they heard about Shkodran Mustafi's late replacement call-up. A central defender? Who has never played in the Bundesliga? For Marco Reus—Germany's great hope for offense? For many, that mystification really lasted until the first World Cup game. But after that it became apparent why Jogi Löw had made the right choice.

Mustafi with the World Cup trophy

Germany's soccer establishment only got to really know him in Brazil. The opportunity had existed much sooner. The son of Albanian parents started to play soccer at 1. FV Bebra. When he played U11 in 2003, he already made regular visits to the DFB basecamp in Bad Hersfeld. In 2006, at the age of 14, he decided to transfer to the Hamburger SV's boarding school and left his parents' home in tranquil Hessia: "There were no opportunities for a soccer career in Bebra, and so I had no choice. My parents stood behind me and have always supported me in all areas. At 14, I was already on my own at the boarding school, was independent early on, and had to make my own decisions."

"I WAS INDEPENDENT EARLY ON AND HAD TO MAKE MY OWN DECISIONS"

Previously at home in offense, he now was retrained as a defensive midfielder and central defender, and during his U19 days, he was invited several times to practice with the pros under then head coach Martin Jol. In 2009, Mustafi was assigned to the German U17 European Championship squad and won the European title with teammates Mario Götze, Marvin Plattenhardt (Hertha BSC), and Marc-André ter Stegen (FC Barcelona). That same year, in spite of other inquiries from Manchester City and Borussia Dortmund, Mustafi decided to take the next step and joined England's FC Everton. About why he made this decision, he says today: "[In Hamburg] the thing [I] missed was the connection with the pro team. The pros were in the stadium, and the youth teams were elsewhere. But at FC Everton, all teams trained on the same grounds. After the pros' practice, David Moyes [then head coach and team manager at FC Everton] went around and watched the U15, U17, etc.

The physical therapists and doctors working for the pros also took care of the youth players. I just had the feeling that I was getting closer."[84] At Everton, Shkodran signed his first professional soccer contract. Mustafi: "When I realized that I had reached my limits at HSV, I wanted to try something new. Everton made major efforts to sign me and showed me a definite athletic prospect. To me, it was a dream come true, and I was eager to play in the Premier League." His soccer role models were also English: "When I still played offense, it was David Beckham, and when I became a defender, it was Rio Ferdinand."

But in the years to come, he was unable to establish himself on the first team and played on the reserve team. Although, from his perspective, it was still an important step: "Another country, a different mentality, a different language, that shaped my character, and I was able to learn a lot from the insane tempo at each practice. But tactics took a bit of a backseat." The biggest culture shock on the island? "I never acquired a taste for English food."[85] He took a step backward and transferred to then Italian 2nd League team Sampdoria Genoa. "That's the beauty of soccer. You never know where it will take you. Back then I told my father: 'From England to Italy—I think there is nothing new left for me.'"[86] The next culture shock hit him in the Ligurian harbor town: "The first time I was on the squad, we lost a home game. Afterward, we couldn't go home for hours because the fans had laid siege to our locker room. At that moment, I sure wondered about the place I had come to."[87] Athletically, the young newcomer also had to wait in line. He spent the

---

84 Biermann, 2015, *11 Freunde* #160, p. 29.
85 Ibid.
86 Ibid.
87 Ibid.

first six months almost entirely on the bench: "To date, that was the toughest time in my career. But the athletic director and the coach wanted to protect me because we were a long way from advancement opportunities. They told me, one error in such a phase, and the fans and the media would immediately write me off, and I may never recover. Back then, I thought it was an excuse, but in hindsight, I am glad. There were players who really suffered from situations like that."[88]

"TO DATE, THAT WAS THE TOUGHEST TIME IN MY CAREER"

But Shkodran Mustafi patiently stayed put and used his chance. The first year after the promotion to the Serie A, the young player had 17 appearances. The following year, he became a permanent fixture in the Sampdoria central defense. "I learned a lot about tactics, became familiar with new systems like the back-three. For a young player, that is an advantage." In March 2013, he made his debut on the U21 national team. During his second year in Italy, he drew a lot of attention with his strong performances, which were also noticed by German national team coach, Jogi Löw. As a result, Shkodran was nominated for the national A team for the first time in February 2014. Despite the fact he had not played one international match for the national A team, Joachim Löw called him up for the preliminary World Cup squad in Brazil. Mustafi celebrated his debut on the national A team at the international test match against Poland. "When you have played on all the U teams and are always looking up, it is an incredible feeling to be invited. A dream came true when I least expected it."[89] But he wasn't considered during the nominations and ended up on the final squad only as a result of offensive player Marco Reus' injury. It was a big surprise to many, but not to Miroslav Klose, who, together with Lazio Rome, had played against him: "Mustafi is the makes the difference on Genoa's defense. His place on the squad is absolutely justified."[90]

---

88 Biermann, 2015, *11 Freunde* #160, p. 32.
89 Friedrich and Mayer, 2014, "Mustafi: An incredible feeling," Interview with Marcus Friedrich and Patrick Mayer from Feb. 28, 2014, *Sport1 Online*. Available at: http://archiv.sport1.de/de/fussball/fussball_dfbteam/artikel_847502.html.
90 *Spiegel Online*. Available at: http://www.spiegel.de/sport/fussball/deutschland-bei-wm-2014-shkodran-mustafi-ist-mister-x-aus-italien-a-971428.html.

Mustafi confirms that Italian soccer can be good schooling, particularly for a young player: "[Italian soccer] is very tactical with lots of players who are older and more experienced, clever foxes. One of them, who I thought was too old and should quit, created lots of problems for me every time because he was so cunning. I'm referring to Antonio di Natale of Udinese, who will be 38 this year. When you zone out for even a second against someone like him or Francesco Totti or Andrea Pirlo, they will play the ball to where it really hurts. Pirlo, especially, knocked my socks off. Watching him on TV, I thought, he's a grandpa, he'll be slow. On the field, you learn that just the opposite is true."[91]

Mustafi was brought on during the first World Cup game against Portugal and, thus, accumulated his first World Cup minutes and lived his dream: "Two years ago, I was standing in front of the screen at Public Viewing back home in Bebra, and now I was suddenly part of the World Cup team on my way to World Cup camp."[92] Mustafi also played 44 minutes in the second game against Ghana. That might have turned into even more minutes if a muscle tear during round 16 had not stopped him. But in spite of the injury, Shkodran was already a regular member of the team: "I did not even realize that I was hurt. The team had such a good vibe that I always felt a part of it. I took part and joined in the excitement. I will never forget the night of triumph. The moment I raised the trophy, so many emotions flooded through me—it is impossible to describe, and it will take time to process it all." Instead of recovering from the strenuous Serie A season on summer vacation, he became world champion on a legendary night in Rio. After the World Cup, Mustafi transferred to FC Valencia in Spain for 8 million Euros, although he had other offers as well: "I wanted to join a club with the prospect of getting UEFA Europa League, or better yet, Champions League experience. Unfortunately, that was not possible in Genoa. But I also didn't want to join a big club where I might not matter. At Valencia, they told me that I wouldn't get a free ride but would be closing a gap in the team. Besides, they showed a lot of interest, called constantly, and inquired after me."[93]

---

91   Bermann, 2015, *11 Freunde*, #160 p. 32.
92   Ibid.
93   Ibid.

*"THE TEAM HAD SUCH A GOOD VIBE
THAT I ALWAYS FELT A PART OF IT"*

Successful with Valencia: Shkodran Mustafi

And Mustafi did not need a free ride. From the start, he made his mark with strong performances and, as the key player in central defense, an integral part of Valencia's team. "As world champion, you tend to walk a little taller on the field, and your self-confidence is huge, but on the other hand, it also raises the pressure because you are viewed differently and have to prove it at every game." Nevertheless, his great success in the summer of 2014 has eased his mind: "I no longer have to agonize over a bungled risky pass. It is what it is, and next time I'll try again."[94]

His performances, of course, generate lots of demand from top European clubs. But Shkodran keeps his feet on the ground–even if there is little time left. "All the years I played in England and Italy, and now in Spain, staying in touch with home is important to me. When I see my former classmates and teammates lead their 'normal' lives, it keeps me grounded and shows me how fortunate I am. I see how my relatives get up at 6am every day, work hard and a lot, and still barely make it. That's the real life. Not the life I live. But I would give up soccer for my family if necessary." He visits his family and friends as often as possible:

94 Ibid.

"On the one hand, it's my job with lots of hoopla, but in the end, I am only human like everyone else. If I play a crappy game today, it's not the end of the world."[95]

"I WOULD GIVE UP SOCCER FOR MY FAMILY IF NECESSARY"

Meanwhile, firmly established on the German national team: world champion Mustafi

---

95   Ibid.

4.3 SEBASTIAN RODE-FROM A PARKING LOT TO FC BAYERN

Sebastian Rode "I learned to prevail against bigger and stronger opponents".

Sebastian Rode did not attend one of the modern youth performance centers, did not go to an elite soccer academy. He did not visit a DFB base camp once a week. "That pushed me forward in the beginning, less so as I got older." He played for the Offenbacher Kickers youth. "Until U19 I sometimes practiced on a hard pitch that was the parking lot for the pro home games." Today he plays for Bayern Munich.

"My parents did not put pressure on me. It was important to me to get my college entrance certificate, but there were people who said I should quit school and focus on soccer." Sebastian Rode is an intelligent young man with good manners. He is shy, friendly, and engaging. But when he steps on the field, something happens: He turns into a tackling machine, a fearless daredevil who captivates with major running ability and action speed. Sebastian Rode is a modern holding midfielder with soccer IQ and vigor. "I was one of the shortest and slightest players in the U15, and to some extent in the U17, and so learned to assert myself against stronger and bigger players."

Having had two major knee injuries at age 20 is not the norm—playing for one of the best clubs in the world even less so. After stints at SKV Hähnlein, FC Alsbach, SC Victoria Griesheim, as well as Darmstadt 98, he switched to the Offenbach Kickers youth division, where he started to practice with the pros during the 2008/2009 season and was brought on twice in his first season. "When I switched to the B Youth, I got an offer from Eintracht Frankfurt, but for their second B team. But I chose Offenbach's B1 because I saw better development opportunities for myself there."

Sebastian Rode at the start of his career

After two years came the switch to Frankfurt, and his career took off. But he had his share of setbacks. In 2009, Rode tore his ACL; a year later he suffered cartilage damage in the other knee. "Those major injuries were tough diagnoses, but the support of my family and friends steadied me, and I focused on school during that phase. Basically that was a welcome distraction."

He did not let these setbacks deter him and since then has been doing special exercises to regain stability. Rode took extra shifts with the athletic coach, which paid off. If he weighed 147 pounds before, five years later it was 161 pounds. "I was given a specially designed fitness regimen by fitness coach Kristian Kolodzai at Eintracht to stabilize both knees and worked very hard. The personal training helped me a lot." The hard work still pays off today: "I have gained muscle mass and stabilized my knees."

Rode made it a habit early on to do more than others. His credo: "That is how I accomplish things." Last winter, when it was certain that he would leave Eintracht Frankfurt, top clubs from all over Europe courted him. He chose what appeared to be the toughest road—the then best club team in the world—FC Bayern Munich.

A decision that is typical of him. Rode remembers: "Back when I switched from Offenbach to Frankfurt, many doubted that I would become a Bundesliga player. There have always been doubters like that in my life, but in the end, I have always managed to prove them wrong." Rode had no such doubts, nor did he harbor any illusions: "In my youth, I didn't worry every day about becoming a pro. I wanted to get better, have fun playing soccer without pressure, but still win every practice game."

When asked about his switch to Munich, he responds confidently: "Many believe that only seasoned pros can make it at Bayern, and I prove otherwise." His response to the question of whether he is at risk of putting on airs: "It is a matter of character, a question of personality type. I enjoy being praised, but I am also self-critical and know that I must continue to work hard on my goals." The people who surround him also do their part: "The people around me keep me grounded: my family, friends, and girlfriend. And the two major knee injuries taught me that things can change in an instant."

"I HAVE ALWAYS MANAGED TO PROVE THE DOUBTERS WRONG"

His goals at Bayern: "I want to play as many games as possible. It wasn't an easy step, but I am ready for the challenge because growth only happens when you are faced with challenges." The new arrival, whom athletic director Matthias Sammer affectionately dubbed "wicked gnome," admits: "I change as soon as I enter the player tunnel; it's true." And as to Sammer's nickname for him: "Wicked gnome is a compliment, a commendation. I think it shows the ability to always hang tough, to not give in, to be assertive, to conquer balls. Those are attributes that sum me up."

Attributes Rode will need on the title champion team. After the first training units, he already noted: "Even at practice everything is two steps faster than at Eintracht Frankfurt, and the tempo is consistently brutal. At practice, all players without exception give 100% all of the time so they will get to play. This continuous rivalry leads to absolute concentration because every player wants to start at the next game. In doing so, you learn a whole lot and improve your technical–tactical grasp which Pep Guardiola demands."

But Sebastian Rode also has a big goal outside of Bayern: "It is important to set goals. My goal is to play on the national team, and Bayern is certainly also a springboard for that." Maybe as soon as the 2016 European Championship.

4.4 DEBUTING WITH A CLUB RECORD- MAXIMILIAN ARNOLD

He made history at age 17

Due to his age, Maximilian Arnold was not admitted to the acceptance test at Dynamo Dresden's sports academy in 2006. Only after a person of authority interceded on his behalf was he allowed to go to Dresden at age 12. Almost 10 years later, Maximilian Arnold has not only experienced a lot, but he has already made history: On November 26, 2012, he played his first Bundesliga game at age 17 and is, thus the youngest debutant in VfL Wolfsburg's club history. His first Bundesliga goal followed in April 2013, again as the youngest player in VfL history. During his first 'real' men's soccer season, he took over the position of playmaker from

Maximilian Arnold

none other than the Brazilian, Diego, who subsequently fled to Atlético Madrid. But the road to that point had been anything but easy.

"Life at the boarding school in Wolfsburg was less difficult than it had been in Dresden. By then I was used to boarding school life, and for the first time I had a private room I could retreat to." Another source of support for Maximilian Arnold has always been and still is his family and his girlfriend. "They gave me support and strength in these situations and helped me regain some much needed

Arnold celebrating with Diego

self-confidence." Arnold has many good memories of the VfL Wolfsburg boarding school: "The boarding school in Wolfsburg left nothing to be desired. It was very new, very clean, very professional—just plain good! I was very comfortable there. Our educators were like mothers and fathers, teachers, and good listeners all in one. They always had a sympathetic ear if you had a problem. At lunch and dinner you saw nearly everyone who lived at the boarding school and were able to talk about everything that happened."

Despite the positive circumstances, Maximilian Arnold was not always free of doubt: "Especially in the beginning, after the switch to VfL, I had misgivings about the choices I had made. But it mostly wasn't fear but rather uncertainty about whether or not I'd be able to make it." Then Arnold threw it into high gear on the Vfl youth teams, and he played. Was playing with older players a problem? "No, I always thought it was great. It was a lot of fun and made me more mature." "Arni," as he was dubbed, did not get impatient about transitioning to the pros: "It was all very well planned: Monday was a day off; Tuesday through Friday I trained with the pros; and on the weekends I practiced with the U19. That did not change until I played regularly with the pros. Later I wanted to play in the U19 championship even though I was already playing for the pros."

"I WAS TERRIBLY SAD AND DISAPPOINTED IN MYSELF"

But Arnold, too, had to suffer some setbacks. When asked about the most difficult phase in his career to date, he responds: "The red card in the first game of the 2013/2014 season. After that I went into a hole. I was terribly sad and disappointed in myself. It felt like I had thrown away my dream of becoming a pro soccer player in the Bundesliga."

But Arnold worked his way out of that hole. About the differences between pro and youth soccer he says: "In youth soccer it's all very amicable; in pro soccer it's about making money, about rivalry and getting to play. As a pro you are much more in the public eye; everything is public knowledge. In youth soccer you can make mistakes; it's not as tough, and the tempo is considerably slower."

Can you have friends in pro soccer? "Yes, I have only soccer friends. It's easy to talk to the soccer players because they know and can relate to my situation and my life."

Arnold has been a part of the DFB's youth national team since the U16. The highlight to date: Coming on in the 76th minute against Poland on May 13, which also resulted in his becoming a national A team player. "It was an absolutely amazing feeling. The anthem, coming onto the field, the coach, the entire staff, everything was amazing! Everyone talked to me from the start, tried to explain things. I am definitely pumped for our next encounter!"

"ARNOLD IS INTELLIGENT, QUICK-WITTED, AND HUMBLE"

Wolfsburg's sports manager, Klaus Allofs, thinks very highly of the man from the own youth: "He can take the path of Mario Götze and Julian Draxler. He has maturity, soccer IQ, and learning ability. Arnold is extremely ambitious and not short on self-confidence." Allofs even compares the "instinctive player"[96] (head coach Dieter Hecking) to Mesut Özil: "Of course there are similarities to Özil. Arnold has a decent amount of self-confidence, is intelligent, quick-witted, and humble." Arnold is definitely not intimidated by big names: "At first it is definitely amazing to play against all of these stars, but it is about the success of the team, and you have to do what it takes to achieve that. It doesn't matter who's standing in front of you."[97]

The young pro describes his other goals like this: "I want to achieve a lot with the VfL, and I want to be back on the national team. I want to further establish myself in the Bundesliga." No doubt his coach at VfL Wolfsburg, Dieter Hecking, will help him do just that: "He is very critical. But that's important for me as a young player. I

Always dangerous: Maximilian Arnold

still have a long road ahead of me." And Arnold wants to continue down that road with gusto and no pressure: "From time to time I just marvel at the fact that I get to play with such players. I don't feel any pressure. I take every situation as it comes and try to make the best of it to be successful."

---

96   *Presseportal.* Available at: http://www.presseportal.de/pm/33221/2454928.
97   *Spox Online.* Available at: http://www.spox.com/de/sport/fussball/bundesliga/1307/News/vfl-wolfsburg-klaus-aloffs-vergleicht-maximilian-arnold-mit-mario-goetze-und-julian-draxler-u-19-nationalspiler.html.

4.5 BACK TO HIS ROOTS– THE PATH OF MARCO REUS

Marco Reus is one of the best soccer players in the Bundesliga, and every top club in Europe has had its eye on him. But by extending his contract at a time when his team went through a difficult phase, he took an unusual stand against the trend in the soccer market. He followed his heart and stayed with Borussia Dortmund, demonstrating his affinity with his home club.

Reus possesses all the elements an offensive soccer player at the highest level must have. He delights the soccer world with his tempo dribbling, his finish, and his free kicks. Reus is a high-speed soccer player who deploys all of his skills: running speed, action speed, anticipation, quickness, and technique. He always looks for the direct 1-on-1, running hard for his team. That is why journalists voted Reus soccer player of the year in 2012. Having debuted for the German national team in 2011, today he is a regular and important member of Joachim Löw's team, who says about the shooting star: "On an international level, it is getting increasingly more important to have players like Reus who look for the direct challenge. He is bold, determined, and a strong dribbler." Reus has grown into a top international player, but few know that the road to this career was also fraught with setbacks, and his path to his dream of becoming a pro soccer player was long and rocky.

Marco Reus was six years old when he joined Borussia Dortmund's youth division. He lived the dream of many children, becoming a member of a team at a youth performance center. With each year, Reus did not only get older, but his hobby of playing soccer for his beloved Borussia gained more importance and more performance pressure. Reus had been with the club for 10 years, having just graduated from the U16, when it seemed like his dream had come to an end. He was rejected due to physical deficiencies. The U17 coach was looking to other players.

Detour via Rot-Weiß Ahlen

Legs like toothpicks, uniform way too big—but in spite of the technical skills he would display time and again, no one trusted in his soccer abilities. "I took a step backward," remembers Reus, who left home to switch to Rot-Weiß Ahlen. There he completed the U17, U19, and even had five appearances with the U23 in the fourth division. After that, Reus became a member of Ahlen's regional league team, which advanced to the 2nd Bundesliga in 2008.

During the 2008/2009 season, he finally saw a breakthrough to pro soccer: After 27 appearances with four goals, he switched to Borussia Mönchengladbach. With that switch, Marco Reus had finally made it to pro soccer. But rather than resting on his alleged laurels, he played two excellent seasons with the Foals before returning to his home club in Dortmund for 17 million Euros through a release clause.

"YOU CAN'T CHILL FOR EVEN A SECOND;
YOU HAVE TO STAY ALERT AND READY"

Next to his outstanding dribbling skills, Reus is also feared for his spectacular free kicks, which, due to his unusual shooting technique, have often resulted in goals. World Cup record holder Miroslav Klose, Reus' former teammate on the national team, is full of praise: "His shooting technique is exceptional." Reus knows that this technique has less to do with talent than hard work: "When I was young, I never had a real behind and did not dare take long-distance shots." Developing this weapon is really the result of years of training.

"I acquired most of my soccer skills on the field," says Reus. Even today, after appearances in the Bundesliga, the Champions League, and the German national team, Reus is never satisfied: "For all of us the challenge is concentrating on the job at hand. You can't chill for even a second; you have to stay alert and ready. The ball you lose is lost by the entire team." For that reason, being diligent every day is completely normal to Reus: "We all work on our weaknesses every day. For instance, I work on my technique, on settling and controlling the ball, and also on my free kicks. The perfect player does not exist."

And he is pretty ambitious, too: "I want to list major titles on my CV." An injury he sustained during the final test game against Armenia prior to the World Cup prevented him from joining the team in Brazil—a particularly bitter pill for Reus. The DFB invited him to the final, but he declined and instead toiled at rehab for his comeback back in Germany. "The first few days after dropping out of the World Cup were extremely difficult because my dream had shattered, but I always try to stay positive." The people in his life help: "It is important to have people around me who stand by me when things aren't going well. Who don't just pat me on the back, but who also issue constructive criticism. That includes my family, friends, and advisors."

A part of the team despite his injury—German national team players hold Reus' jersey

An important aspect of his personality is his grip on reality, which doesn't let him forget where he comes from in spite of the daily hubbub around his person. "Of course I make mistakes, too. That's normal. In spite of my development in recent years, I have not changed much, and I won't do so in the future."

For Reus, the chance for the next big title will be at the 2016 European Championship in France, where he will hopefully raise the trophy, fit and healthy, with his buddy Mario Götze.

PART 3: EXAMPLES

5

INDIVIDUAL TRAINING UNITS OF STAR PLAYERS

As a pro with Bayern Munich, VfL Wolfsburg, Valencia, or Borussia Dortmund, you train with the team on a daily basis. In addition to the national championship, international appearances in the Champions League or Europa League, as well as with the national team, make for lots of games each year and a very tight schedule. Still, even at the highest level, the previously mentioned pros want to continuously work on their weaknesses and strengths so they can improve and support their teams. Each player's goal is to be as successful as possible. That only happens with constant training in which processes are automated so they can be applied situationally in a game.

The players demonstrate that requirements for individual positions definitely differ and that they must pay attention to even the smallest detail. At this high playing level, it constitutes the critical difference which, in the end, will result in preventing a goal, preparing a goal, defending an advantage at the end of a game, or scoring.

Ultimately, each training unit improves skills each and every day.

Of course, the players also have individual training programs to improve their physical strength. But on the field is what matters most, and for that reason, the players will show you their "best of" exercises that can be easily replicated.

5.1   RALF FÄHRMANN

Ralf Fährmann is a homegrown Schalke player who left his home in Chemnitz at age 14 to move to the youth boarding school in Gelsenkirchen. In 2006, he became German national champion with the U19, and today he is not only the undisputed number 1 in goal, but also one of the role models at Schalke. Next to his amazing parries, Ralf's popularity with his fans is also due to his forthright and cheerful disposition, which is well received in the Ruhr region. Moreover, on the field, he embodies the ambition, diligence, and absolute will to improve. We are delighted that Ralf was willing to share a few key aspects of his training.

"Today's goalkeeping is very complex and has different requirements. Of course, the most important part of goalkeeping is clearing balls to prevent goals. But commanding the penalty area and joining in possession as well as intercepting opposing counters play a major role. Below are some favorite exercises that I regularly complete with my goalkeeping coach. I take the old adage 'you play the way you train' very seriously and am extremely motivated at every practice."

Attention to detail

Orientation: "In different situations, such as a cross outside the box or a lateral shot, I have to orient myself as to where I need to stand to make the angle of my goal as small as possible for the attacker."

Offensive thinking: "Whether with crosses during the game or opposing corners, I get in an anticipatory crouch to intercept the ball if necessary."

Transitions: "After a cross has been intercepted, the accuracy of the throw-out or punt is important for the initiation of a counter."

Pressure: "When the opposing offense approaches, I still need the composure and the technique to ensure possession with a well-aimed pass or a volley."

Please note the following abbreviations: GC = Goalkeeping coach, RF = Ralf Fährmann, CF = Center-forward.

1. The first exercise emphasizes agility, explosiveness, power, and reaction ability. I sprint from one of the posts to the different colored cones at top speed while the goalkeeping coach throws or kicks a ball in the opposite direction. The exercise is made more difficult because I don't know at what moment I have to parry the ball or its trajectory (the ball is thrown and kicked from different angles).

2. It is my goal to intercept the ball after crosses from different positions. As I do so, I have to keep an eye on the dummies that are in my way. The timing of coming out and jumping has to be perfect. Variation: One player also jumps to impede Fährmann slightly.

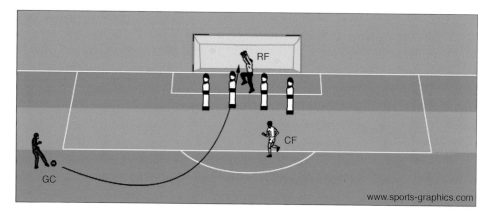

3. Supplementary exercise to exercise 2. Depending on the situation, a quick continuation of play is required after gaining possession. After catching the ball, immediately transition with a throw-out into diagonally positioned mini goals (pole goals as an alternative) or to a teammate.

4. The coach feeds me a pass. Here the first touch is very important. I play a volley, ideally with the second touch, into a bounded area (from both sides). It is important to pay attention to the speed of the ball. Contest with point system.

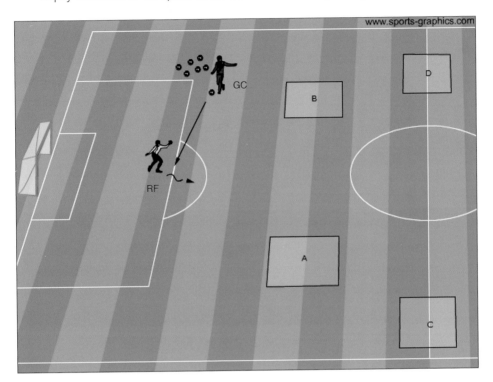

5.2 SHKODRAN MUSTAFI

"The position of central defender requires different skills. When the opponent has the ball, it is important to close off the center and protect and defend the own goal. When the opponent plays high balls, you need strong header skills; when the ball is played low, it's important to win the ball on the ground. In this position, we are also responsible for buildup during possession. That means using different passing techniques to prepare and initiate an attack. I regularly practice all the different options."

Attention to detail

Anticipation: "It is important to explore the possibility of reaching the ball before the forward and intercepting the pass. If that isn't possible, it is important to keep a distance to the forward (basketball defense distance) so he is unable to use his body to turn around against you, and you can then no longer get to the ball."

Aggressiveness: "Of course, the opponent should feel through physical contact that you are determined to get the ball. But you have to be careful, particularly in and around the penalty area, so as not to provoke a free kick or penalty kick."

Crosses from outside: "In this situation, there is no zone defense. Instead, I have to stand close to the man to keep the forward from getting the ball."

Buildup: "Due to the opponent's possible pressing variations, it is important to master different shooting techniques that must be practiced regularly. Next to passing, you must also be able to take long, accurate shots."

Exercises

1. In a 1-on-1, pass to a forward who has his back to the goal; the objective is to prevent the finish.
   When he turns, position your body between the ball and opponent to get possession (ideally without a foul). Win the ball with a run rather than an unnecessary tackle! Mark an extended 6-yard area that the forward is not allowed to leave.

Please note the following abbreviations: GK = Goalkeeper, SM = Skodran Mustafi, CF = Center-forward, MF = Midfielder, OM = Outside midfielder.

Variation B: The penalty box is extended so the forward has more room.

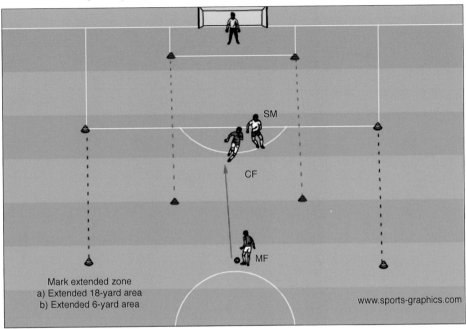

Mark extended zone
a) Extended 18-yard area
b) Extended 6-yard area

www.sports-graphics.com

2. Cross from outside with forward in the center. It is important to both keep an eye on a) the player who made the cross and b) be close to the opponent to be able to defend. Here good timing of a defensive header is necessary as well as smart use of the body to get to the ball before the opponent does. After a few crosses or feeds, the player crossing the ball switches sides.

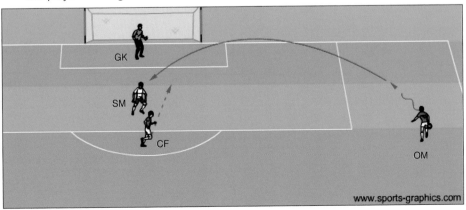

www.sports-graphics.com

3. Mark a certain area where the ball must land. After a pass and quick ball control, the volleys are played into these specific target zones with buildup on both sides. Play with points—competitive mode.

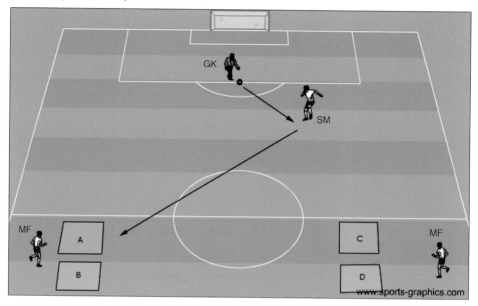

4. With two players and limited touches (no more than three), contest using two parallel cone goals that the ball must be passed through. Play for points: one point for a pass through each cone goal—contest. Change directions to use both feet.

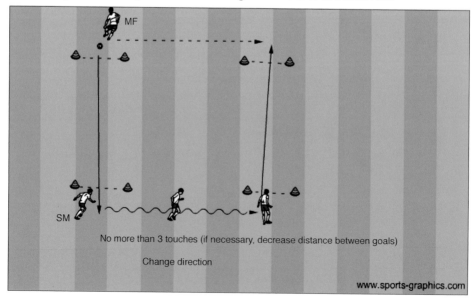

No more than 3 touches (if necessary, decrease distance between goals)

Change direction

www.sports-graphics.com

5.3   SEBASTIAN RODE

"During buildup and transition, the space is especially tight in the center, and there is little time during possession. That's why it is important to practice and automatize different situations to be able to make the right decisions in the game against the opponent as well as pressure of space and time."

Attention to detail

Move to get open: "It is important to gain a time advantage over the opponents, meaning tempo and timing have to be right."

Open body position: "I look over my shoulder to get an overview and then position myself in space so I can view the field to create a quick consecutive situation."

Settling and controlling the ball: "The first touch must be in the direction of movement to avoid loss of time. For this reason, I practice from both sides to train both feet."

Passing sharpness and accuracy: "Precision is more important than sharpness. Once you are confident, you increase the passing tempo. Not every ball finds its target. That's why you practice."

Please note the following abbreviations: SR = Sebastian Rode, F = Forward, CD = Central defender, DEF = Defender.

Exercises

1. Two teammates each have a ball at their feet. I approach diagonally and with my first touch take the ball in my direction of travel. After taking the ball, I play a pass into one of the three cone goals. Alternate sides to train both feet!

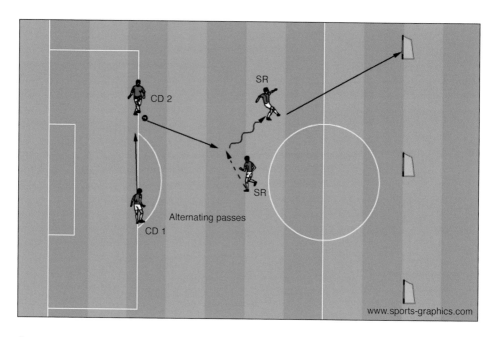

2. Perform the procedure as exercise 1, but the teammate who passes the ball calls out which mini goal to pass to. This results in decision-making and action speed but is still fun and motivating.

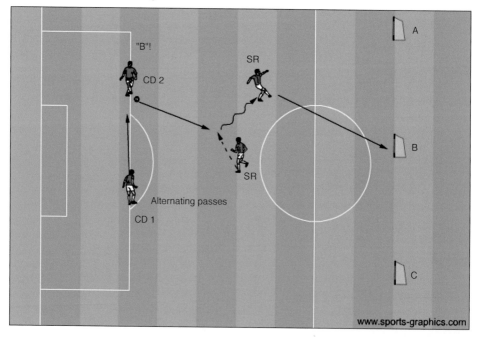

3. From deep to deep: I receive a pass from CD (1). With my first touch I am in the open position; the forward (2) chooses a running lane between cone goals where I play a precise pass to his foot.

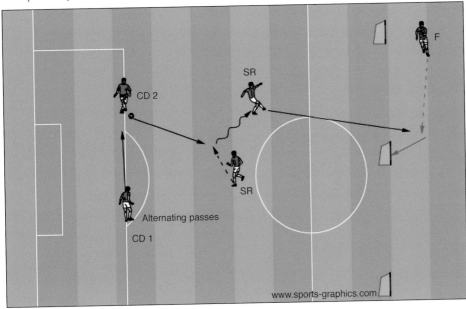

4. From deep to deep: Perform exercise 3 but with an additional defender. I must get out of the opponent's cover shadow and play a pass into the seam to my deep-lying teammate.

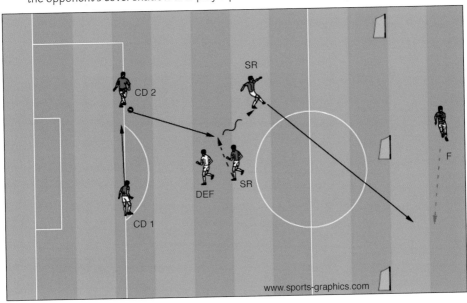

5.4 MARCO REUS

"The importance of set pieces was particularly apparent at the World Cup. I mentioned that I used to not be able to shoot very well, and only through practice, practice, and more practice did I work on my weaknesses. Of course, today I am happy every time I succeed in a game. I try to automatize the sequences again and again and pay attention to every detail."

Attention to detail

Concentration: "I position the ball and try to calm myself and control my breathing to be able to focus on the free kick or corner kick."

Step sequence: "I perform a certain sequence of backward steps to achieve my best timing for the strike against the ball."

Observation: "I look up at the wall and the goalkeeper and determine whether I will lift it over the wall or put it in the corner of the goal."

Run-up angle to the ball: "I run up at a certain angle to get the best touch on the ball."

Point of contact on the ball: "How I make contact with the ball is important. If I make contact near the bottom, it creates a different trajectory than when I strike it closer to the top."

Purposeful use of technique: "When I make contact with the ball, I don't follow through but rather decelerate at the right moment to create an unpredictable trajectory."

Marco Reus taking a free kick

Please note the following abbreviations: MR = Marco Reus, F = Forward, CF = Center-forward.

Exercises

1. Lateral free kick in different end zones (variations) with two dummies as the wall, one forward, and one goalkeeper. Vary exercise with an additional defender and an additional attacker.

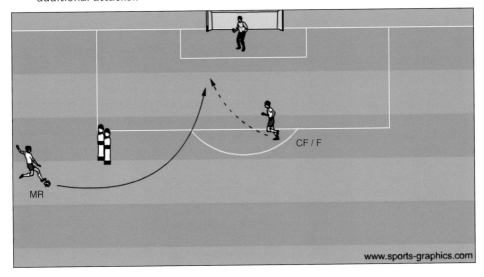

2. Practice a direct free kick from a central position with dummies and goalkeeper.

3. Practice a left corner shot on the goal with four different end zones. Vary exercise with one attacker in the target zone.

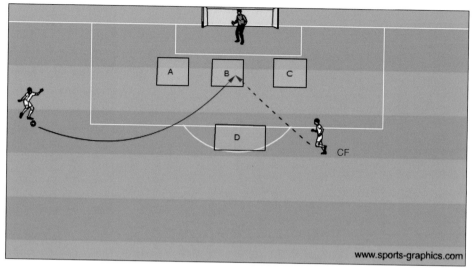

4. Practice a left corner away from the goal with four different end zones.

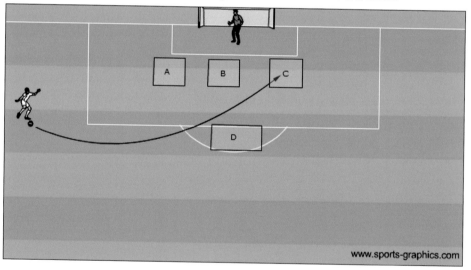

PART 4: AMATEUR SOCCER

6
RECREATIONAL SPORTS FORM THE BASE OF THE PATH TO THE TOP-AMATEUR SOCCER

Every Monday morning, at thousands of workplaces, people analyze the previous day's Bundesliga games, celebrate the goals, debate controversial referee calls, and root for their favorite club. The attention on pro soccer clubs from the media and fans is omnipresent. But, ultimately, this enormous presence is bestowed on only a very small portion of the soccer world. The majority of people who are active in soccer are volunteers and members of an amateur club and are not in the limelight.

They pursue the most beautiful pastime in the world and support children, adolescents, or a men's team in various capacities. They paint the lines on the field, are coaches, manage the club funds, or fulfill other important functions within the club. They donate their limited free time and strength (and occasionally their nerves) to the team and respective club. Without the active participation of these people there would be no amateur soccer games. Their commitment supports children and adolescents in pursuing a meaningful recreational activity as well as learning and internalizing social behavior.

After the 2014 World Cup, thousands of enthusiastic children in clubs all over Germany wanted to emulate their role models and each weekend wanted to score their own personal goal of the year. But the clubs were unable to meet this huge demand because the availability of locker rooms and training grounds, the number of quality coaches and helpers, and the reasonable organization of practice and games were often not feasible.

In Germany, amateur soccer stirs the masses. More than 6.5 million members are organized under the umbrella of the DFB and are members of approximately 25,500 clubs and more than 165,000 teams. Last season, 1.8 million soccer games were played in Germany—an average of 5,000 games per day. In other words, if soccer were played on all 52 weekends a year, there would be 34,615 games per weekend.[98]

1.7 million volunteers in clubs that offer soccer invest 120 million hours of labor per year for the sake of their children's love of soccer or because they enjoy the companionship. The annual added value is 1.8 billion Euros.

If the national team and the professional leagues project the magic of German soccer inward and outward, the amateurs are the heart and a large part of the soul.

Former DFB president, Wolfgang Niersbach, emphasizes this: "Without the amateurs as a broad base, we at the top would not be this successful with the national team."[99]

While professional soccer achieves record numbers year after year and the DFB shines in the glory of the national team, many small clubs fight for their survival. One of the main problems in most places is that the clubs lack older up-and-coming players. The condition of many fields, locker rooms, and showers is often disastrous.[100]

---

98   *DFB Online*. Available at: http://www.dfb.de/news/detail/dfb-von-a-bis-z-massenbewegung-amateurfussball-56117.
99   Ibid.
100 *ZDF Zoom*. Available at: http://m.zdf.de/ZDF/zdfportal/xml/epg/20310993,befc0476-9f54-36cb-bcb9-43012ec8ac62.

A big supporter of volunteerism—former DFB president, Wolfgang Niersbach

For many clubs, with or without tradition, it has become a daily struggle for survival. The problems are many and varied: declining memberships, fewer sponsors, and outdated or nonexistent infrastructure. The existence of many clubs is threatened; changing demographics as well as changes in the recreational behavior of children and adolescents contribute to the problems soccer clubs have in maintaining their broad offerings.

According to a DFB statistic from 2014, more than 13,000 youth soccer teams discontinued their operations in the past six years.[101]

This is a particular challenge for many sports clubs today. "The basis for our soccer is volunteerism. German soccer would not have its associational status without the admirable commitment of its many volunteers. It must remain our collective duty to promote and support volunteerism," says former DFB president, Wolfgang Niersbach. League president, Dr. Reinhard Rauball stresses: "Every volunteer has my utmost respect for his personal commitment to amateur soccer!"[102]

In order to reinforce this sentiment, the DFB and the regional associations published a master plan in 2012 for the future strategy of amateur soccer. The main objective is to secure the future of amateur soccer.[103] The master plan's implementation is meant to further improve the image and self-conception of amateur soccer, modernize its operations as needed, and augment the overall service offerings for the clubs' staff members.[104]

Also pivotal here is the overall strengthening of volunteer commitment in amateur soccer. This is already being done through the DFB's image campaign, as well as in the modified Internet platform, FUSSBALL.DE.

---

101 *Phönix Online*. Available at: http://www.phoenix.de/unsere_amateure_echte_profis/849354.htm.
102 *DFB Online*. Available at: http://www.dfb.de/vereinsmitarbeiter/jugendleiterin/artikel/danke-ans-ehrenamt-stadionbesuch-zum-internationalen-tag-des-ehrenamtes-1158/.
103 *DFB Masterplan Amateurfußball*, p. 4f. (PDF from June 15, 2014).
104 Ibid.

Club services will be expanded. Next to additional practice offers for coaches, offerings in soccer club management that can be used by board members are also being created.[105] In the future, these will become more flexible to keep up with current developments in game planning and operations. This will take place through different kinds of competitions, flexible game planning, smaller teams, as well as more opportunity for players to play for an older team if there is a lack of team strength or to appear for another team in their own age group without having to change clubs. The introduction of a *fair play league* is also becoming increasingly common in German soccer associations.[106]

With regard to qualifying and introducing adolescents to volunteerism, the DFB launched their project *Junior Coach* in 2014. The goal is to provide students with a basic soccer-specific education that can serve as the first module for a national C license in recreational soccer. The hope here is the early procurement of volunteer soccer talent.[107] In this regard, the junior coach training program is already getting support from Bundesliga clubs on the local level.

Therefore, the DFB is not abandoning amateur clubs, but is trying to purposefully create improved conditions in amateur sports through the *master plan's* quick implementation so that the next soccer generation may also be served.

---

105 *DFB Masterplan Amateurfußball*, 2014, p. 6f.
106 Ibid.
107 Ibid.

6.1 STARTED SMALL, MADE IT BIG—SOME NATIONAL TEAM PLAYERS AND THEIR BEGINNINGS

What do the names TSV Pähl, FC Oberaudorf, or TSV Pattensen mean to you? Surely only experts will know the answer.

These three clubs have one thing in common: They are the home clubs of three 2014 world champions. And without the amateur clubs, there would hardly be any national team players, because world champions begin their careers at amateur clubs:

WORLD CHAMPIONS WHO STARTED THEIR CAREER AT AMATEUR CLUBS		
Westfalia 04 Gelsenkirchen	Mesut Özil (Arsenal London)	
FT Gern Munich	Philipp Lahm (Bayern Munich)	
TV Oeffingen	Sami Khedira (Juventus Torino)	
Greifswalder FC	Toni Kroos (Real Madrid)	
SG Blaubach Diedelkopf	Miroslav Klose (Lazio Rome)	
FC Oberaudorf	Bastian Schweinsteiger (Manchester United)	

WORLD CHAMPIONS WHO STARTED THEIR CAREER AT AMATEUR CLUBS		
TSV Pähl	Thomas Müller (Bayern Munich)	
TSV Pattensen	Per Mertesacker (Arsenal London)	

Niersbach: *"The 25 current German national team players were trained at 65 different clubs. That is a fascinating overall performance."*[108]

Horst Hrubesch, current U21 national team coach, extols the amateur base: "We must work to bring more licensed coaches to the base, whereby it must be said that the volunteers in the small clubs make our national team players! That is where the foundation is laid. And the more fun the young players have, the more is offered to them, the better they will become."[109]

But the issue of fewer volunteers has also become apparent in the area of youth professional soccer. Dr. Jens Rehhagel, director of Hannover 96's youth performance center, stresses: "This issue is a current problem for us as well. Not all the staff at our club is full-time. We have helpers or lower-level coaches who work for the club on a volunteer basis. Of course, working for a Bundesliga club has its appeal, and for many, devoting their weekend to soccer is normal. We are in the fortunate position of having people who want to donate their time to Hannover 96, but we don't take it for granted. And we are well aware that it can be different at other smaller clubs."

Prominent examples can also be found in the area of coaching. At the beginning of his Budesliga coaching career, André Breitenreiter coached U8 Juniors at TUS Altwarmbüchen. Ralf Rangnick got his start as coach in a district league (SC Victoria Backnang).

---

108 *DFB Online.* Available at: http://www.dfb.de/news/detail/dfb-von-a-bis-z-massenbewegung-amateurfussball-56117/.
109 *Fußballwoche Berlin Online.* Available at: http://fussball-woche.de/artikel/talent-allein-ist-nicht-entscheidend/.

Need some more examples? Here they are:

FROM AMATEUR COACH TO BUNDESLIGA COACH		
TSG Salach	Markus Gisdol (formerly TSG 1899 Hoffenheim)	
Delbrücker SC	Roger Schmidt (Bayer 04 Leverkusen)	
TSG Leonberg	Robin Dutt (formerly VfB Stuttgart)	
SV Straelen	Jos Luhukay (formerly at Bertha BSC)	

The DFB recruits volunteers.

6.2 PROJECT TUS HALTERN– A DIFFERENT KIND OF AMATEUR CLUB

Initial situation in 2008

The club had lots of the kinds of problems many other amateur clubs have: a lack of solvency, a decline in membership numbers, unfilled positions for officials and coaches, a lack of commitment from sponsors, ailing infrastructure, and a lack of equipment. Add to that an understandable lack of athletic success.

Christoph Metzelder, who grew up in TuS Haltern's youth soccer program and maintained contact with his home club after becoming a pro, returned to his roots. The club in which Christoph and Malte Metzelder, Sérgio Pinto, and Benedikt Höwedes also became Bundesliga pros and German national team players—making it unique in Germany for a club of its size—was reorganized.

But anyone who thought that the name Metzelder would create a second "Hoffenheim" through significant donations was absolutely wrong. Ronald Schulz, head of the soccer department, shakes his head at such a scenario: "Christoph is not an investor or patron of the club. It is not a matter of money but rather conceptual work, of providing his knowledge and work at the club with dedication and passion as project manager with a social mandate."

Metzelder shares this view and adds: "The club will not be padded with money, but rather will develop organically and at some point will become self-sufficient within its refinancing structure. We are making purposeful investments in infrastructure and training. The magic word is sustainability."

Reframing

He drove the reframing of the club forward by assembling a new team of experts. The ultimate objective was to bring about a professionalization in the area of intermediate amateur soccer. A financial expert, a marketing expert, and manager for the soccer department were hired.

Christoph Metzelder and Ronald Schulz

For the implementation, a short- and mid-term catalogue of strategic measures was created:

- Correcting the financial imbalance
- Professional financial and tax management
- Targeted media and public relations work
- Filling vacant coaching positions
- Reactivating volunteer commitments
- Acquiring sponsors
- Member recruitment
- Soccer-specific structural improvements

During the years of development, four strategically important points were addressed that, on the one hand, were meant to highlight the project's sustainable approach and, on the other hand, significantly increase the quality of training.

153

TuS Haltern's development pyramid

Infrastructure:

- Install an office as place of business
- Convert the cinder field to third generation synthetic turf
- Renovate the second grass field
- Set up a central ball room for all teams
- Purchase tilt-resistant junior and senior goals
- Ensure optimal field maintenance

Equipment:

- All teams play in uniform jerseys
- Design club's own gear catalog
- Cooperate with a regional supplier of team sporting goods
- Cooperate with sporting goods manufacturer
- Replenish new training materials

Training:

- Increase coaching certification training rate
- Offer certification free of charge
- Organize basic coaching course in Haltern

- Hold internal training courses and conferences
- Establish a voluntary year of social service
- Ensure that innovative and age-appropriate youth training will be offered in the future and that talented players and coaches have opportunities for advancement
- Create and solidify a training philosophy for the club that is developed by coaches and takes into account the performance level of children and parents

Marketing:

Across Germany in the form of a first marketing campaign by a former regional league player

Mix of communication:

- In the form of classic modules:
  - press kit, flyer, stadium newspaper
  - series of articles in the coaching magazine fussballtraining
- Image campaign 2009

Haltern has a lake. FROM THE TEARS OF OUR OPPONENTS.

Haltern is the gate to Munsterland. BUT WE DON'T LET ANY PASS.

There is no industry in Haltern. BUT WE CRANK OUT GOALS LIKE AN ASSEMBLY LINE

Interactive communication:

- Homepage
- Social media platforms like Facebook®, Twitter®, and Instagram®
- TuS TV
- YouTube® channel
- Television documentaries and reports

These measures will increase a deep regional rootedness and identification while at the same time allowing the club's fellow campaigners to meet their social responsibility.

TuS chairperson, Christoph Metzelder, says: "We want to strengthen and preserve the club's family atmosphere, get parents more involved in the project, and hope to gain support from many local and transregional sponsors."

And **athletic successes** have materialized:

- In 2010, both senior teams advanced.

The interim results seven years later:

- After his professional career, Christoph Metzelder has become active as assistant coach for juniors and seniors, supports the athletic management for soccer, periodically helps out as an active participant on senior teams, and as of July 2014, is now the presiding chairman of the entire club.
- Over the years, the membership of the entire club has changed greatly (approx. 1,100 members), but the soccer department is now bursting at the seams with 550 members and 20 active teams. Many new teams (5) have been formed, particularly in the areas of mini-kickers, U8, and U11.
- With membership numbers at athletic clubs in the area generally decreasing, these steady numbers can be considered a success.

The quality of coaches has increased significantly

The soccer department currently has 15 certified coaches with national C to A licenses, meaning there is a nearly 100% licensing rate among coaches. For a recreational sports club, this is definitely something special, if not unique.

TuS Haltern's guiding principle is that athletic successes are a logical consequence of a professional environment. And that is what happened here. The first and second senior teams have already advanced two consecutive times in four years.

But subsequently, a robust economic development was no longer able to keep up with the athletic advances. By now, the youth teams have also celebrated their first small successes. But here it takes much longer to make up for the educational failings of the past.

A place for a voluntary year of social service?
Since 2008, TuS Haltern has offered one opening each year for a voluntary year of social service in sports. This position is sponsored and supervised by the State Athletic Association of North-Rhine Westphalia. During that time, adolescents or young adults can explore youth athletic coaching at TuS Haltern, make contacts, assume responsibility for children, and get some initial professional experience at the business office. To date, every social service volunteer has immediately found or been offered an apprenticeship after their 12 months of service.

In 2004, TuS Haltern, in association with a private college in Bochum, offered for the first time a position for a six-semester dual sports management course of study, meaning that the student would spend two days each week studying business administration at the college while also working 20 hours per week at TuS Haltern's business office at the training company, as well as taking on his or her own area of responsibility.

Another example is the integration of a disabled team. This is made possible through cooperation between TuS, the social welfare agency, and a team from the Sheltered Workshops and is successful. The team is the German national champion.

Rising attendance numbers?
In everyday league life, independent league attendance has not increased significantly and has leveled off at 100 to 200 per game day—with the exception of local derbies against teams from nearby, when approximately 400 to 600 spectators flock to the grounds.

Thus, Haltern, with a population of 35,000 and 8 (!) soccer clubs, simply has too many games on the weekends at various locations. However, special games and events, such as the jubilee game against Schalke 04, the game against the students from the soccer instructor training course, and games against Borussia Dortmund, regularly draw 1,000 to 3,000 spectators.

Approximate social media numbers?

The main communication paths are through the TuS homepage (approx. 40,000 visitors per month) and the club's Facebook page with currently 7,615 fans. That is a phenomenal communication platform for an amateur club of this size. At this time, there is simply a lack of personnel to operate any additional forms of social media.

Increased sponsorship?

Since 2008, the number of sponsors has increased 100%. At this time, TuS Haltern has 50 to 80 local, regional, and national sponsors who are involved on a regular basis.

What does volunteer staff involvement look like?

Volunteer activity consists primarily of current or former participants from the soccer department who stay involved after their active careers. For instance, youth players from the older youth teams coach mini-kicker teams and U8 players and help with soccer camps. Players form the "old timers" take on administrative duties (e.g., enroll and unenroll players, youth leaders, treasurer). Others are active on the board or in sponsorship acquisition or support.

More important than athletic success is the fact that the club has managed to reinvent itself. It is palpable. Here volunteerism is all about commitment and a coming together in the heart of the west; here a community was created, and this club is exemplary in many ways, or as Metzelder puts it:

"EVEN THOUGH I PLAYED IN THE BIGGEST STADIUMS IN THE WORLD,
THE STAUSEEKAMPFBAHN STADIUM HAS ALWAYS REMAINED MY FAMILY ROOM."

PART 4: AMATEUR SOCCER

7
BETWEEN BERNABEU, ARENA BERLIN, AND STAUSEE-KAMPFBAHN STADIUM–

INTERVIEW
WITH VICE WORLD CHAMPION,
CHRISTOPH METZELDER

Christoph Metzelder was vice world champion with the German national team in 2002 and played for Borussia Dortmund, Real Madrid, and Schalke 04. Today he works for pay-TV channel *Sky*. But his heart belongs to TuS Haltern.

Christoph Metzelder

> Today you can look back on a successful career by far. At age 19, you were still with the Preußen Münster regional league; at age 20, you were a Bundesliga regular in Dortmund; and at age 22, you were vice world champion with the national team. As a young player, how did you process this rapid rise?

"I graduated from high school in 2000, and three months later found myself at the Westphalia Stadium, playing my first Bundesliga game. But back then I wasn't really aware of the contrast because at Borussia Dortmund I 'grew into' my job from the first day on. My first time in the locker room with Matthias Sammer, Jürgen Kohler, Stefan Reuter and co. was exciting, but after a couple weeks, I was a member of the team. You learn a lot with every game and every training unit. That's why, from my perspective, it wasn't really that rapid. The pace I felt was clearly different from that perceived on the outside. I was fortunate to become a pro at a time when there were still definite hierarchies, and seniority prevailed. The older and more experienced players set the tone; the younger players listened and learned. Next to my upbringing, that is what kept me humble and gave me a realistic view of things. To put it bluntly: If I had shown up at practice in a Porsche, Stefan Reuter would have single-handedly retuned it the very next day."

"AS A YOUNG PLAYER I NEVER WOULD HAVE SHOWED UP IN A PORSCHE"

> During the "rumble period" around the turn of the millennium, Germany looked primarily to other countries for its continued development. During your time in Spain at Real Madrid from 2007 to 2010, how was German soccer viewed and rated there?

"With lots of respect, whereby it was most likely aimed at the outcome orientation. The way we as the German team focused on points at the big tournaments and were able to produce good results was associated with typical German virtues like discipline, fighting ability, and strong will. But that thinking changed after the 2006 World Cup. The player development that has continued impressively all the way to the World Cup title in 2014 got noticed."

> How is Spain's philosophy different?

"Spanish players have good technical training. All of their clubs have mastered positional play and short passes. But in my opinion, the golden era of Spanish soccer between 2008 and 2012 is synonymous with FC Barcelona's dominance at the club level, which took place at the same time. During that time, the Spanish national team was largely shaped by FC Barcelona protagonists like Puyol, Pique, Xavi, Iniesta, and co."

Christoph Metzelder at practice with Real Madrid

> You have played with Cristiano Ronaldo and Sergio Ramos, to mention just a couple top players. These superstars are adored by millions of people. What was that like for you as their teammate?

"The atmosphere in the Real Madrid locker room was always very relaxed in spite of so many, in some cases quite eccentric, individualists. Even with 20 national team players, everyone knew what he had to do. Sergio Ramos and Cristiano Ronaldo are two absolutely exceptional athletes—outstanding soccer players, but unbelievable athletes. Both have the physical stamina that allows them to play 60 mandatory games per season and the drive that makes the difference in today's elite soccer.

In Cristiano's case, in addition to predisposition, there is also an incredible amount of ambition. His behavior on the field may sometimes appear self-centered and occasionally sulky, but it reflects his expectation to always be the best."

> During your professional career you were considered a "thinker" who regularly excogitated and scrutinized himself and those around him. How did that benefit you as a player?

"Strategy is more important for my position as defender than it is for the offense. Next to one's own performance, that must viewed as the big picture; the work of the back four combined with the goalkeeper and the defensive midfield and also the strategic direction of the entire team are enormously important. Otherwise, too much cogitating on the field is not helpful. Quite the opposite! Soccer is extremely intuitive and decisions must be made every second. Brooding does not help here!"

"SOCCER IS EXTREMELY INTUITIVE. BROODING DOES NOT HELP HERE."

> Over the course of your career, you experienced repeated throwbacks due to serious injuries. How do you come back strong, and how do you process these setbacks?

"Only in retrospect do I now see that time clearly. In the end, a serious Achilles tendon injury cost me a portion of my career and permanently arrested my development. Until then, I had been German national champion at age 21, vice world champion, and one of the most promising talents in Europe in my playing position. And I was able to still play pro soccer for nine more years, including for Real Madrid and at two big international tournaments. The facts show that my handling of setbacks and the always-recurring fighting spirit are a part of my résumé and also of my personality."

> You have publicly criticized the soccer business. In your opinion, what has changed in recent years?

"Soccer has developed into a global business in which the players as protagonists have become their own brands that radiate far beyond the green turf.

But with the increasing medialization and digitization, players have themselves become senders of messages. This is a major challenge to the team bond. Hierarchies break away; communicating in social networks has become more important than in the locker room. That creates a different player, and by extension, different team profile. Combined with still rising salaries and transfer fees, it is my opinion that soccer must be careful not to leave behind the middle class. This sport has always thrived on the idea that theoretically one can show up at a practice and shake the hand of his favorite player. Social networks suggest an extreme closeness—being very close to the lives of the players—which in reality is completely untrue. With their behavior and lifestyles, the protagonists actually manage to create an ever-greater distance between themselves and their fans."

> **After your career, you took on new areas of responsibility. What are they?**

*"Next to my work as an expert for pay-TV channel **Sky**, I am the managing partner for the advertising agency Jung von Matts/sports. It gives me the opportunity to shine a light on the sports and soccer business from the marketing and communication side. Since 2006, I have also been working with the Christoph Metzelder Foundation for disadvantaged children and adolescents in Germany and for the past six years have also been supporting my home club TuS Haltern."*

> **What are the fundamental differences between an amateur club and a professional club?**

"Everything is, of course, smaller and less business-like; many processes are broken down but yet very similar. You work with people—in an amateur club, they are mostly volunteers—who must be enthused and motivated, and must also be informed of decisions and, if need be, must be criticized. I actually have all of these essential duties on a daily basis in a professional club. With all the complexity, what matters most there as well is to manage people and interest groups every day anew."

*"SELF-AWARENESS AND SELF-EVALUATION
ARE CRITICAL IN SPORTS"*

> How do you motivate young players even when they will most likely never have a big career?

"Self-awareness and self-evaluation are critical in sports. In my opinion, it has become more difficult because there are more external influences, and pro soccer as a goal is so alluring. The increasing medialization and digitization brings you so close, but the path there is extremely rocky, as it has always been, and in the end is denied the vast majority of up-and-coming players. But in amateur soccer, too, it is about playing in the district league or the regional league. And I am always shocked at how much the self-awareness differs from objective observation. In a team sport, in particular, I should be able to notice if I am not able to compete in that group. But self-evaluation is often different."

> How important do you consider amateur work?

"We always talk about the base and how important it is for German soccer. Amateur soccer is the starting point of every sport and soccer career. I played pro soccer for 13 years, but I played youth and amateur soccer for 18 years. During that time, you not only lay the foundation for your continued career, but even earlier than that, it influences your decision as a child of which sport you want to engage in long term. I came to soccer at age 6 through a friend from Kindergarten and stuck with it, although I also did gymnastics and track and field at the same time. Thus, the responsibility of amateur soccer to get children excited about this sport is immense and can only be met locally at Germany's more than 26,000 amateur clubs. It takes more than 6 million amateur soccer players to be able to train the 23 world champions of Brazil! And amateur soccer is also the fan base of pro soccer. Every amateur soccer player is both a fan and a consumer. Therefore, this group is also extremely important from an economic standpoint."

> *"AMATEUR SOCCER HAS THE RESPONSIBILITY*
> *TO GET CHILDREN EXCITED ABOUT SOCCER"*

> What is the appeal of coaching at an amateur club?

"It is original work that has nothing to do with the business end of pro soccer. In amateur soccer, I have to depend on the gratuitousness of my players. With all-day schools and a diverse range of sports, cultural, and recreational activities, I have to motivate them to practice 3 times a week and show up to play on Sunday mornings. It is a big challenge, but also incredibly empowering when you are able to get these young people excited. And when they actually implement what you have tried to teach them, it is enormously satisfying."

> How do you motivate young people to become volunteers?

"It is increasingly more difficult and has certainly become a societal problem. Work is more and more linked to financial incentives. Doing something purely out of a desire to help or organize is becoming a rare phenomenon. The coaching allowance gives us the opportunity to create a small financial incentive, but classic volunteerism will always be important because many clubs simply don't have even that money. In my experience, clubs must try to get their own youth involved as early as possible. Older youth players take over mini-kickers or U8 teams. People who learn to volunteer early on and are directly exposed to it often continue to do so permanently."

> Youth performance centers emphasize holistic training. In your opinion, how important is that for a young player?

"In my opinion, it is an attempt to create 'perfect soccer players' who are able to survive in modern soccer, not only athletically, but also as public and media figures. The argument that an opportunity is also given to those who are not able to make the leap, I think, is a flimsy argument. Any player who goes to a youth performance center wants to become a pro soccer player. And even if there is cooperation between schools, the amount of time required and the motivation make it obvious: complete focus on soccer! Soccer clubs cannot have a genuine interest in becoming catch centers for those who don't succeed. They create the perfect framework to train tomorrow's pro soccer players. They invest in the players so they will produce the best-possible performances for the club during that time."

PART 4: AMATEUR SOCCER

8
A LOOK AHEAD

"In the end, ambition, tenacity, volition, and sacrifice are still the decisive criteria at a young age, when you want to establish yourself as a pro. That hasn't changed and will continue to be the key to success in the future as well."[110]

–Sebastian Kehl

"Today's structures and training of young players at the DFB work extremely well. Germany is a few steps ahead of us. Germany will dominate European soccer in the next 10 years."[111]

–Willy Sagnol

Willy Sagnol gained an insight into the German structures during his former functions as athletic director for the French association and as a U21 coach. He, therefore, is able to draw a comparison to France; he inferred dominance for some years.

110 *11 Freunde Online.* Available at: http://www.11freunde.de/artikel/wie-sebastian-kehl-profi-wurde/page/.
111 *11 Freunde Online.* Available at: http://www.11freunde.de/interview/willy-sagnol-ueber-die-equipe-tricolore-und-die-nationalelf.

"I remember an interview with Arsène Wenger from 2000. Wenger thought that due to training and colonization, France would have a 10-year head start, particularly in Europe. And yet the German concept completely overran that of the French. We learned from them and then did it better. Now we have to continue to work on ourselves."[112]

–Volker Finke

Volker Finke, who coached for many years at SC Freiburg and is jointly responsible for the sustainable structures of the training club, praises Germany's progress, but also recommends caution.

Where is training headed in the coming years? Who trains the world champions of tomorrow? Those questions, as shown by the two quotes, are the subject of a hot debate and cannot be answered with 100% certainty. Who speaks for what position? Who speaks against it? And exactly how will it happen? Following, we hold this debate in the form of two commentaries.

8.1 "GERMANY WILL DOMINATE EUROPEAN SOCCER IN THE NEXT 10 YEARS"

The entire soccer world looks to Germany with justifiably great interest, and many use the German recipe for success in youth and elite soccer player development as a model for lasting improvements of their own structures. During the summer of the 2014 World Cup in Brazil, the entire world was able to marvel at the results of exemplary talent development. By now, even top European clubs like Arsenal London use German training as a model. Even in Brazil, simply the soccer nation, the professionalization of structures based on the German model is being considered. Around the world, Germany's talent development system is considered exemplary. Next to an outstanding infrastructure, which can be seen in the absolutely top-notch youth performance centers, the German Soccer Association and the German Soccer League have managed to create a system that

---

112 Quote from http://www.morgenweb.de/sport/fussball/streich-schickt-schone-grusse-an-red-bull-1.1818689.

will ensure—through a tight-knit network (starting with supportive measures at the district and association level such as DFB base camps) and permanent quality management (certification and licensing)—that Germany with its national soccer team will remain a part of the world elite for years to come. A statement by Borussia Dortmund's youth performance center director, Lars Ricken, underscores this assertion: "With its system of a junior Bundesliga, the DFB junior club competition, the regional cups, as well as the DFB and association selection process, I see Germany as extremely professional and well positioned. I suppose we may be the envy of the world."[113]

Germany's 7-1 victory against Brazil at the 2014 World Cup

Another important element is the extremely high-quality training of coaches. Matthias Sammer, at that time DFB sports director who accompanied the positive development, stated it very succinctly: "More than ever the head coach is the key and the measure of all things."[114] As of 2015, the new DFB B license was introduced to further optimize the training of coaches in Germany. With that, additional work is being done to continue the training of highly qualified coaches for youth performance soccer.

In an organization that is respected worldwide, young players do not only receive outstanding technical training, but typically German traits like discipline and winning mentality are not neglected, as the German national youth team's successes show. Germany

---

113   *DFB Online*. Available at: http://www.dfb.de/news/detail/lars-ricken-deutschland-wird-weltweit-beneidet-120438/.
114   *DFB Online*. Available at: http://www.dfb.de/news/detail/matthias -sammer-trainer-ist-schluessel-und-mass-der-
      dinge-11649/.

won the European title with the U19 in 2008 and 2014 and with the U21 in 2009 and 2013. These successes show that the next title generation is already in the starting blocks. The pillar of personality development with its educational and psychological guidance will continue to bring up players with solid character traits in the future. The examples of top stars like Manuel Neuer, Marco Reus, and Sebastian Rode make clear that even in the future, these characteristics will still be seen as essential to achieving a long-lasting professional career.

In addition, many German coaches continue to think outside the box. Without looking to the Dutch technical schools and the existing talent development in France, England, and Spain, Germany would never have been able to pull ahead in the fast lane.

The influence of foreign coaches like Lucien Favre, Pep Guardiola and Louis van Gaal has already enriched German soccer and provided food for thought.

A team cannot demonstrate its strength more clearly than Germany did during the semi-finals at the 2014 World Cup when host country Brazil with all its superstars and outstanding technical skills was outclassed. The team is another factor. The 2014 World Cup title was everyone's success, not only the team's and the entire coaching staff's or the whole operational team's. No, it was a title for the youth performance centers because no other country's breadth of training is as extensive as Germany's. More than 60 clubs participated in the training of the 23 Brazil world champions.[115]

So not only did the national team and Bundesliga coaches share in this fantastic success, but also the youth performance center coaches, and let's not forget the dedicated volunteer recreational soccer coaches, in particular, who made this title possible with their blood, sweat, and tears.

Even with all the success at the top, the base was never forgotten—the origins of the world champions. The DFB did not forget the recreational and amateur sport, but rather supports it with targeted programs, so players who may not be able to make the leap to the very top can be retained so they can raise the quality of their league and lay a new foundation for a new generation at their home club with their volunteer commitment.

---

115 *DFB Online*. Available at: http://www.dfb.de/u-19-junioren/news-detail-u-19/schmieden-der-europameister-hier-wurden-unsere-u-19-talente-ausgebildet-101972/.

The DFB is already trying to figure out how to maintain the world-class niveau of German players and, of course, to improve it. Löw adds: "We are just now working on the 2015/2016 master plan. We want to develop new ideas, find new solutions. Because soccer is constantly evolving, and we have to take that into account."[116] Another element could be the planned DFB training center, which is slated for completion in 2018 and already trailing behind, as France has already built one in 1988, England in 2012, and Spain has had one since 2004.

The beauty of soccer is that no one is unbeatable. But this is certain—and here we completely agree with Willy Sagnol—with its foundation of excellent quality, its system of sustainability, its technical strength paired with typical German attributes, the German national team will definitely be at the top of the world for the next 10 years.

8.2 MORE INVESTMENT TO STAY ON TOP

"Wenger thought that because of its training and colonization, France had a 10-year head start over everyone else in Europe. And yet the German concept still completely overran that of the French."

Many others have been at this juncture and thought themselves invincible. The Hungarian national team in 1954 after being undefeated for two years, the French at the turn of the millennium, and most recently the Spanish. The following statistic may surprise many who are optimistic about German training. The International Center for Sports Studies (CIES) scrutinized talent development efforts in the five top European leagues of Spain, England, Germany, Italy, and France.[117] FC Barcelona ranked highest; German clubs ranked quite a bit lower. At the top of the rankings is FC Barcelona's talent development program, which has 13 players from their own youth on its squad. Furthermore, 30 players who were trained at the famous La Masía soccer academy play in Europe's five major leagues. German clubs do not reside in the upper rankings. FC Bayern Munich is ranked 17th (6+14), VfB Stuttgart is ranked 20th (7+10), followed by Schalke 04 (9+7).

---

116 *ZEIT Online.* Available at: http://www.zeit.de/news/2014-12/26/fussball-joachim-loew-arbeiten-am-masteplan-201516-26125604.

117 *Fußballtransfers Online.* Available at: http://www.fussballtransfers.com/andere-ligen/top10-diese-klubs-bilden-am-erfolgreichsten-aus_48802.

TOP TWELVE (NUMBER OF HOMEGROWN PLAYERS ON THE SQUAD; IN PARENTHESES ARE THE NUMBER OF PLAYERS TRAINED ON THE MAINLAND)		
1.	FC Barcelona	13 (30) ➝ 43
2.	Manchester United	12 (24) ➝ 36
3.	Real Madrid	8 (26) ➝ 34
4.	Olympique Lyon	15 (18) ➝ 33
5.	Paris St. Germain	5 (22) ➝ 27
6.	Athlético Bilbao	15 (9) ➝ 24
6.	Real Sociedad	15 (9) ➝ 24
6.	Stade Rennes	5 (19) ➝ 24
9.	Girondins Bordeaux	11 (11) ➝ 22
9.	RC Lens	9 (13) ➝ 22
9.	FC Arsenal	7 (15) ➝ 22
9.	Atalanta Bergamo	5 (17) ➝ 22

Anyone who stops improving stops getting better! We can all remember Franz Beckenbauer's statement after the World Cup win in 1990. He said: "The German national team will be unbeatable for years to come."[118] Ten years later, the legendary "zero hour" took place at the European championship in 2000. The debacle of the German national team epitomized by a "group of pensioners" who produced hideous amateur soccer, prompting the world to laugh at Germany.

---

118 *Fußballtransfers Online.* Available at: http://www.fussballtransfers.com/andere-ligen/top10-diese-klubs-bilden-am-erfolgreichsten-aus_48802.

Anyone who thinks the Germans will make the same mistake twice is certainly wrong. But anyone who believes that the 2014 World Cup was the "changing of the guard" of Spain's dominance is hugely mistaken. Spain won the last U21 European championships in 2011 and 2013 and the U19 in 2007, 2011, and 2012. The next generation of Xavis, Iniestas, Iker Casillases, and Sergio Busquets is chomping at the bit. That is also why the Spaniards did not react with the customary reflexive managerial changes after their disastrous World Cup. Successful coach Vicente del Bosque is still in office, and, moreover, he can absolutely rest assured he will remain there, because the next generation of excellent players is waiting in the wings. And that's just Spain! The Netherlands, as a much smaller country than Germany, develops top players year after year.

In France, too, a hopeful new generation is growing up. France has also changed its structures with regard to the European championship in France and changed the national team squad. France won the 2013 U20 world cup with Paul Pogba as captain, who is considered one of France's emerging superstars. Finances also played an important role. With the newly negotiated media contract in the Premier League, teams will push forward into new dimensions. That can certainly impact the quality of up-and-coming players. Schalke's youth performance center director Oliver Ruhnert confirms this based on the experiences he has had, and the discussions that were initiated at the English association in order to raise the homegrown talent quota within the individual teams could bring about a significant boom in English soccer.

A new generation of superstars is growing up: Paul Pogba (left), Raheem Sterling (center), and Eden Hazard (right)

There are no secrets in the age of globalization and the Internet. These days, even the small countries like Gibraltar, Armenia, and San Marino know how a back four operates. Countries like Belgium and Switzerland, and also Austria have made huge strides in talent development, and the effect was already apparent at the last World Cup. In many ways, the German training approach focuses on winning. By doing so, technically strong but physically not fully developed players sometimes fall by the wayside. Not all of them are able to jump back, as the example of Marco Reus shows. But when looking at the youth national teams of other nations such as Spain, one notices enormous differences in talent selection and style of play. Sometimes short-term success hampers long-term development.

On the soccer market, the world's elite rapidly focuses on Europe. But anyone who thinks that the Brazilians, who have been part of the absolute elite for more than 50 years, won't have a role to play in world soccer in the future is barking up the wrong tree. Soccer players have been and still are Brazil's number one export product. No other country can compare to the number of Brazilian players with outstanding training. When closely observing Brazilian soccer players, one notices extreme differences that other nations may never decode. As previously noted, other nations are preparing to challenge us in the years to come. Surely this competitive contest will strengthen the desire to continuously improve.

He put everything to the test at the start of his time at FC Bayern and searched for permanent improvements: Pep Guardiola

When Pep Guardiola became coach at Bayern Munich, the team had just won the triple. Guardiola began by putting everything to the test and to make changes where needed.

Success requires the most changes. German soccer has to do some work if it really wants to remain unbeatable in years to come.

Because this book cannot encompass every subject in detail, we were unable to address certain topics. We asked questions that could be examined more closely in the future:

What happens in recognized talent development programs in Europe such as Sporting Lisbon, Ajax Amsterdam, or FC Barcelona that can be compared to the youth performance centers in Germany?

Will the operational teams at training facilities continue to grow? Are there more personal trainers, a possible top-talent coach, and more experts for the medical and physical therapy staff?

Are there any innovations in the area of conceptual training to manage pressure from the opponent, space, and time, such as working with a visual coach?

To use a very common soccer truism: In soccer, sometimes everything happens very quickly. Because this sentence is full of truth and because we don't want reality to overtake and overrun us, we would like to, here and now, look around in all directions so we may continue to find new perspectives. In the future, one of the biggest challenges will be to improve youth development even more so that Germany will retain its exemplary talent development program for future soccer generations. Let us hope that more talent from individual sources will continue to successfully shoot up to the top in the future.

We are coming to the end, and the following statements speak for themselves:

"The clubs have realized that investing in their youth is, on the one hand, a matter of prestige, but on the other hand, for many clubs, it is a matter of necessity. Because they noticed that there are talented adolescents who will make the jump to the pros if they are given the opportunity."
–Klemens Hartenbach, Freiburg sports director, personal communication, 2009

"If you give your all, you'll have no regrets."
–Dirk Nowitzki

"As soon as you have learned something, you should become a student again."
–Gerhart Hauptmann, author (1862-1946)

REFERENCES

- Armonat (2012). *DFB-Pokal – Reus: Ein Fall für die Wissenschaft.* Vom 19.12.2012. https://de.eurosport.yahoo. com/news/dfb-pokal-basler-reus-fall-f%C3%BCr-wissenschaft-143415295.html

- *BILD Online*: Arjen Robben kritisiert junge Spieler: Nach einem Spiel denken sie, sie haben es geschafft. Vom 15.02.2015. http://www.bild.de/sport/fussball/bayern-muenchen/arjen-robben-kritisiert-junge-spiel-er-39778086.bild.html

- *Bundesliga Homepage:*

  - DFL-Fragen: http://www.bundesliga.de/de/dfl/fragen-zur-liga/

  - Arsène Wenger: Verliebt in den deutschen Fußball. Vom 18.02.2014. http://www.bundesliga.de/de/wett-bewerbe/champions-league/news/2013/verliebt-in-den-deutschen-fussball-arsene-wenger-fc-arsenal.php

- *DB-Magazin Mobil-Online:* Waldherr in: „Manuel Neuer: Unsere Nummer 1". Mobil – Deutsche Bahn Magazin. http://mobil.deutschebahn.com/leben/unsere-nummer-1/

- *DFB-Homepage:*

  - „Danke ans Ehrenamt": Stadionbesuch zum Internationalen Tag des Ehrenamtes. http://www.dfb.de/vereinsmitarbeiter/jugendleiterin/artikel/danke-ans-ehrenamt-stadionbesuch-zum-internationalen-tag-des-ehrenamtes-1158/

  - *DFB-Ausbildungskonzeption*   (http://fussballtraining.com/blaetterfunktion/ausbildungskonzeption/ index.html#/1/zoomed)

  - *DFB-Eliteschulen* (http://talente.dfb.de/index.php?id=518840)

  - *DFB für beste Nachwuchsarbeit in Europa ausgezeichnet* (http://www.dfb.de/index.php?id=500014&tx_dfbnews_pi1%5BshowUid%5D=20992&tx_dfbnews_pi4%5Bcat%5D=70)

  - *DFB von A bis Z: Massenbewegung Amateurfußball.* Vom 16.03.2014. http://www.dfb.de/news/detail/dfb-von-a-bis-z-massenbewegung-amateurfussball-56117/

  - Jensen (2014). Interview mit Fabian Wohlgemuth: Wolfsburgs Anspruch, Spiel zu dominieren. Vom 11.06.2014. http://www.dfb.de/news/detail/wohlgemuth-wolfsburgs-anspruch-spiel-zu-dominieren-58765/

  - PDF *Masterplan Amateurfußball.* Abzurufen u. a. über http://www.bremerfv.de/fileadmin/Down-loads/Masterplan/Masterplan.pdf

  - *Lars Ricken: „Deutschland wird weltweit beneidet".* Vom 07.08.2014. http://www.dfb.de/news/detail/lars-ricken-deutschland-wird-weltweit-beneidet-102438/

  - *Matthias Sammer: „Trainer ist Schlüssel und Maß der Dinge".* Vom 23.07.2007. http://www.dfb.de/news/detail/matthias-sammer-trainer-ist-schluessel-und-mass-der-dinge-11649/

- *Schmieden der Europameister: Hier wurden unsere U 19-Talente ausgebildet.* http://www.dfb.de/u-19-junioren/news-detail-u-19/schmieden-der-europameister-hier-wurden-unsere-u-19-talente-ausgebil-det-101972/

- *Talentförderung* (http://talente.dfb.de/index.php?id=519131)

- *DFL* (2011). 10 Jahre Leistungszentren: Die Talentschmieden des deutschen Fußballs. Diverse Artikel.

- Die *Welt Online* vom 28.12.2013: Premier League-Chef begeistert vom deutschen Fußball. http://www.welt.de/newsticker/sport-news/article123356007/Premier-League-Chef-begeistert-von-deutschem-Fussball.html

- *„Die ZEIT" – Print & Online:*
  - *„Die ZEIT" Online*: Quäl dich, Körper. In Zeit „Wissen" 03/2006. http://www.zeit.de/zeit-wissen/2006/03/Sportpsychologie.xml/seite-3
  - *„Die ZEIT" Online*: Reschke: FC Bayern darf kein „Talente-Verleih" werden. Vom 13.01.2015. http://www.zeit.de/news/2015-01/13/fussball-reschke-fc-bayern-darf-kein-talente-verleih-werden-13085605
  - *„Die ZEIT" Online*: Faller und Kemper 2013: Der Trainer mit den dünnen Beinen. Vom 31.10.2013. http://www.zeit.de/2013/44/fussball-sc-freiburg-trainer-christian-streich
  - *„Die ZEIT" Online*: Joachim Löw: „Arbeiten am Masterplan 2015/16". Vom 26.12.2014. http://www.zeit.de/news/2014-12/26/fussball-joachim-loew-arbeiten-am-masterplan-201516-26125604
  - Wochenzeitung *„Die ZEIT"*, Ausgabe Nr. 19 vom 05.05.2011

- Documents by *ITK*:
  - Sammer (2009). Auf dem Weg zur Weltspitze: Anforderungen an DFB-U-Nationalspieler. *ITK* 2009.
  - Schott (2010). Talentschmiede als Erfolgsfaktor: Auswertung der DFB-Nachwuchsförderung mit Blick auf die WM 2010. (*ITK* 2010)
  - Schoukens, Van Hoecke, Simm & Lochmann (2008). Die Zertifizierung der Leistungszentren 2007-2008. *ITK* 2008.

- Eichler (2013). *„Ich habe so einen Helferinstinkt".* In *FAZ Online* vom 09.03.2013. http://www.faz.net/ak-tuell/sport/fussball/manuel-neuer-im-gespraech-ich-habe-so-einen-helferinstinkt-12107565-p3.html?printPagedArticle=true#pageIndex_3

- *11 Freunde:*
  - Biermann (2015). in *11 Freunde* #160, März 2015, S.28-33.
  - Joswig (2013). Willy Sagnol über die »Équipe Tricolore« und die Nationalelf. Jogi Löw ist der perfekte Trainer! Vom 06.02.2013. http://www.11freunde.de/interview/willy-sagnol-ueber-die-equipe-tricolore-und-die-nationalelf

- Kehl (2015). Wie Sebastian Kehl Profi wurde. „Unsere Generation verschwindet". Vom 08.04.2015. http://www.11freunde.de/artikel/wie-sebastian-kehl-profi-wurde/page/1

- Küppers (2014). Einmal Super-Talent und zurück: Reinhold Yabovom KSC. „Ich fühlte mich sehr cool". Vom 11.04.2014. http://www.11freunde.de/interview/einmal-super-talent-und-zurueck-reinhold-yabo-vom-ksc

- Kuhlhoff (2013): „Fußball ist nie langweilig". Vom 01.03.2013. http://www.11freunde.de/interview/manuel-neuer-ueber-den-bvb-motivation-und-john-mcenroe

- Wiedemann (2008). „England ist Längen voraus". Spielanalytiker Clemens im Interview. http://www.11freunde.de/interview/spielanalytiker-clemens-im-interview

- Feldhoff (2014). *Top 10: Diese Klubs bilden am erfolgreichsten aus.* Vom 28.10.2014. http://www.fussball-transfers.com/andere-ligen/top10-diese-klubs-bilden-am-erfolgreichsten-aus_48802

- *Financial Times Deutschland Online*: UEFA zeichnet DFB-Nachwuchsarbeit aus. http://www.ftd.de/sport/fussball/nationalmannschaft/:uefa-zeichnet-dfb-nachwuchsarbeit-aus/50028845.html

- *Focus Online* 08.11.2010: „Leistung ist planbar". http://www.focus.de/sport/mehrsport/sport-leistung-ist-planbar_aid_569812.html

- *Fußballtraining* – Ausgabe 09/14 *Fußballwoche Berlin online*. Hein (2013). „Talent allein ist nicht entscheidend". Vom 10.06.2013. http://fussball-woche.de/artikel/talent-allein-ist-nicht-entscheidend/

- Gartenschläger & Schramm (2009). Warum Löw den DFB-Kickern Beine machen will. *Welt Online:* http://www.welt.de/sport/fussball/article3427689/Warum-Loew-den-DFB-Kickern-Beine-machen-will.html

- Haid (2013). Fußball ist eine ehrliche Sportart. Ralf Rangnick im Gespräch. *Stuttgarter Zeitung Online* vom 25.10.2013. http://www.stuttgarter-zeitung.de/inhalt.ralf-rangnick-im-gespraech-fussball-ist-eine-ehrliche-sportart.7d4bac3f-5831-4549-a5da-a7e623a6329c.html

- *Hamburger Abendblatt Online* vom 04.05.2012: Borussia Dortmund 2012: Bester Meister aller Zeiten? http://www.abendblatt.de/sport/article106547061/Borussia-Dortmund-2012-Bester-Meister-aller-Zeiten.html

- Hartmann (2008). In den Händen eines Buben. In *SZ* vom 10.12.2008. http://www.sueddeutsche.de/sport/schalke-in-den-haenden-eines-buben-1.868236

- Hoeltzenbein & Selldorf (2014). „Ich spiele auch gern im Feld mit". In *SZ Online* vom 10.09.2014. http://www.sueddeutsche.de/sport/manuel-neuer-im-interview-ich-spiele-auch-gern-im-feld-mit-1.2123221

- Homepage Bayer 04 Leverkusen: *Bayer 04 meldet U23 nach der Saison vom Spielbetrieb ab.* Vom 23.04.2014. http://www.bayer04.de/B04-DEU/de/_md_aktuell-dt.aspx?aktuell=aktuell-10171

- Internetseite WM 2014-Nachrichten: *DFB-Team mit viertjüngstem Kader der WM-Geschichte.* http://www.wm-2014.net/zahlenspiele-dfb-team-durchschnittsalter-von-258-jahren-1235494.html

- Jahrbuch Manuel Neuer Kids Foundation: http://www.neuer-kids-foundation.de/tl_files/downloads/Jahrbuch.pdf

- Kellermann & Schahidi (2012). „Der Charakter schlägt am Ende meistens das Talent". *RP Online*. http://www. rp-online.de/sport/fussball/borussia/der-charakter-schlaegt-am-ende-meistens-das-talent-aid-1.3120084

- *kicker-Sportmagazin* und *Kicker Online:*

  - *kicker-Sportmagazin* vom 26.05.08, S. 44.

  - *kicker-Sportmagazin* vom 27.10.2014, S.13. Interview Benedikt Höwedes: „Viele Talente ruhen sich aus"

  - Lustig (2015). Gladbach: Von der Vision zur Wirklichkeit. Eberl erntet die Früchte seiner (Jugend-)Arbeit. Vom 07.01.2015. http://www.kicker.de/news/fussball/bundesliga/startseite/618528/artikel_eberl-erntet-die-fruechte-seiner-%28jugend-%29arbeit.html

  - Röser (2013). Preetz: Hertha muss auf die eigenen Talente setzen. Vom 27.07.2013. http://www.kicker.de/news/fussball/bundesliga/startseite/589855/artikel_preetz_hertha-muss-auf-die-eigenen-talente-setzen.html

- Klüttermann (2014). *Bayer 04 darf seine U23 abschaffen*. Vom 25.03.2014. http://www.fupa.net/berichte/bayer-04-darf-seine-u23-abschaffen-135986.html

- Kreft & Wimmer (2014). Der große Junioren Report. So gut sind die Talentschmieden der Bundesliga. BILD zeigt das geheime Ranking der Leistungszentren. *BILD Online* vom 15.04.2014. http://www.bild.de/sport/fussball/fussball-bundesligen/so-gut-sind-die-talent-schmieden-der-bundesliga-35352394.bild.html

- Kübler (2014). Manuel Neuer: „Vom Fußballplatz sehe ich nichts". In der *Badischen Zeitung* vom 26.05.2014. http://www.badische-zeitung.de/f-wm/manuel-neuer-vom-fussballplatz-sehe-ich-nichts--85373015.html

- *Mannheimer Morgen*: Müller (2014). Streich schickt schöne Grüße an Red Bull. Vom 31.07.2014. http://www. morgenweb.de/sport/fussball/streich-schickt-schone-grusse-an-red-bull-1.1818689

- Manuel Neuer Homepage: http://manuel-neuer.com/#aktuelles

- Näher (2010). Spanien bleibt der Maßstab. *Schwarzwälder Bote online*: http://www.schwarzwaelder-bote.de/inhalt.interview-mit-bundestrainer-spanien-bleibt-der-massstab.8cb5b7cb-b301-4d29-8a7e-4cfaa3ceb1eb.html

- *Phönix Online*: http://www.phoenix.de/unsere_amateure_echte_profis/849354.htm

- *Presseportal* vom 20.04.2013: Hecking vermisst beim VfL den „durchschlagenden Erfolg". http://www.presse-portal.de/pm/33221/2454928

- Rosentritt (2014). „Ich bin also kein Thomas Müller". In *Der Tagesspiegel Online* vom 08.07.2014. http://www. tagesspiegel.de/sport/wm-2014-halbfinale-deutschland-brasilien-manuel-neuer-ich-bin-also-kein-thomas-mueller/10165396.html

- Schmalenbach 2014: Ohne ihn wäre Neuer aussortiert worden. TZ-Online vom 01.03.2014. http://www.tz.de/sport/fc-bayern/ohne-matuschak-waere-neuer-aussortiert-worden-meta-3392044.html

- Schlüter 2014 bei *Sportbild Online*: U19 Triumph: Ein Titel ohne Bayern. Vom 31.07.2014. http://sportbild. bild.de/meine-meinung/2014/meine-meinung/u19-triumph-ein-titel-ohne-bayern-37062756.sport.html Stand: 22.06.2015

- *Spiegel Online*. Ahrens (2014). Neu-Nationalspieler Shkodran Mustafi: Mister X aus Italien. Vom 24.05.2014. http://www.spiegel.de/sport/fussball/deutschland-bei-wm-2014-shkodran-mustafi-ist-mister-x-aus-italien-a-971428.html

- *Sport Bild Online* vom 04.02.2015: Der brutale Kampf um die Talente. http://www.genios.de/presse-archiv/artikel/SBIL/20150204/der-brutale-kampf-um-talente/131648960.html

- *Sport1 Online* 2011: Neuer: Gomez am Herzen, Kahn im Hinterkopf. Vom 04.06.2011. http://archiv.sport1.de/de/fussball/fussball_dfbteam/artikel_414077.html

- *Spox Online*: Rosige Zukunft vorausgesagt. Allofs vergleicht Arnold mit Götze und Draxler. Vom 29.07.2013. http://www.spox.com/de/sport/fussball/bundesliga/1307/News/vfl-wolfsburg-klaus-allofs-vergleicht-maximilian-arnold-mit-mario-goetze-und-julian-draxler-u-19-nationalspieler.html

- *Süddeutsche Zeitung Online* vom 14.07.2014: Löw: Dieses Glücksgefühl wird für alle Ewigkeit bleiben. http://www.sueddeutsche.de/news/sport/fussball-loew-dieses-gluecksgefuehl-wird-fuer-alle-ewigkeit-bleiben-dpa.urn-newsml-dpa-com-20090101-140714-99-01274

- *Tagesspiegel Online*: Hermanns (2014). Hertha BSC und der Nachwuchs. Drei Sterne und viele Fragezeichen. Vom 22.02.2014. http://www.tagesspiegel.de/themen/hertha-bsc/hertha-bsc-und-der-nachwuchs-hertha-trainer-luhukay-verfolgt-das-prinzip-fordern-und-foerdern/9520570-2.html

- *TAZ Online*. Wedig (2014). DFB-Elf ist Weltmeister. Über Jahre hinaus unschlagbar? Vom 14.07.2014. http://www.taz.de/!5037703/

- *T-Online* (2014). Abschaffung von U23-Teams. Jürgen Klopp: „Das ist eine Katastrophe". Vom 04.08.2014. http://www.t-online.de/sport/fussball/id_70503172/abschaffung-der-u23-teams-fuer-juergen-klopp-eine-katastrophe-.html

- Wallrodt (2015). Neuer ist fantastisch, Ronaldo wie ein Alien. In *Die Welt Online* vom 08.02.2015. http://www.welt.de/sport/fussball/internationale-ligen/article137215594/Neuer-ist-fantastisch-Ronaldo-wie-ein-Alien.html

- Wallrodt (2015). „Mein bestes Spiel war ein 0:0 gegen Freiburg". In *Die Welt Online* vom 27.03.2015. http://www.welt.de/sport/fussball/bundesliga/fc-bayern-muenchen/article138840793/Mein-bestes-Spiel-war-ein-0-0-gegen-Freiburg.html

- *WAZ Online*: Wilhelm (2013). Schalkes Nachwuchscoach Elgert ist „Lehrer, Ausbilder, Förderer". Vom 11.02.2013. http://www.derwesten.de/sport/fussball/s04/wir-muessen-demuetig-bleiben-id7603310.html

- *ZDF-Zoom* vom 11.06.2014: http://m.zdf.de/ZDF/zdfportal/xml/epg/20310993,befc0476-9f54-36cb-bcb9-43012ec8ac62